Handwriting Analysis Dictionary

Handwriting Analysis Dictionary

How to Identify and Rate
the Intensity of Personality
Traits That Can be Found
in Handwriting

(Second Edition)

Lorraine Owens

Kaleidoscope-Kansas City

Price: $24.00

Order from: **Kaliedoscope**
1524 Crystal
Kansas City, Mo. 64126

I dedicate this book to my friend and partner in business, Connie Allen, who is a constant source of inspiration and joy to me.

INDEX

Lorraine L. Owens, Master Certified Graphoanalyst; B.A. in Psychology; listed in *Who's Who of American Women* (1981-82 Edition); President of Kaleidoscope Industries Corp.; partner of Allen and Owens. Past President of Missouri Chapter, International Graphoanalysis Society (1971 and 1977); Recipient of the President's Certificate of Merit Award, 1980; seminar speaker to other state chapters; Graphoanalysis experience includes personnel work, expertise in the field of learning disabilities, personal and compatibility reports, and work with a psychologist at the Kansas State Prison. Teaches Psychology 103 at the International Graphoanalysis Society annual Congress in Chicago, Illinois. Author of *Different Ways to Describe Traits.*

Introduction

When I travel around the country conducting seminars and talking with my fellow handwriting analysts, I feel that many do not have a good grasp of precisely what a trait looks like in writing. In my opinion, this in-depth knowledge of trait identification is the basis upon which a good analysis is written. I find that the analysts who are successful have this knowledge of the traits at their fingertips.

If you cannot identify and measure the difference in heights of the t-stem (pride, independent, and vanity), or clearly have in mind the person who will make every minute count (conservative), or recognize the time-waster (generosity to self), then the personality will be put back together in a way that will not be accurate. This dictionary helps you identify traits and their intensity in the writing quickly.

When I decided to put together this dictionary, the thought crossed my mind as to why this has not been done before, as most handwriting analysts that I know have a "notebook" in which he or she has organized his notes into a useable, practical encyclopedia. But now that I have completed this work I think I know the reason why: it was a large undertaking....but a very rewarding one, I hasten to add.

One of my goals in completing this book is to aid my fellow analysts in becoming accurate analysts and yet, spend less time doing an analysis. I chose a binding that lays open for easy use, and also left room for you to add your own notes and illustrations, so that you could make the book a basis for your own resource manual. The traits listed in the book that do not have illustrations are ones that I could not find in my files. Perhaps you can, from your handwriting files, find a sample of writing that accurately illustrates a trait, for example bluff, indifference, or timid. Rating the traits on a scale of 0 - 10, thereby setting an intensity number by a trait, can be difficult and I believe this book can help you solve this problem.

My method of putting this book together is as follows: The traits are listed in alphabetical order and described with "key" words in the definition underlined. The trait is then illustrated by my drawings and given a rating from 0 to 10. Specimens of writing from my personal files further illustrate the trait. If the trait is a primary trait or an evaluated trait, this has been noted. Some traits are seen in the writing by a primary stroke and can also be evaluated through a combination of traits; both ways have been listed.

Then comes the intensifiers and reductives to a trait, and the opposites, when that is possible. I find this a good method of getting a grasp on a trait. That is, if you think in terms of a trait and its opposite: for example, poise vs. impulsive, broadminded vs. narrowminded, ultra conservative vs. generosity to self, ambition vs. self underestimation.

Also included is a trait chart where all the traits are briefly defined and their intensity is illustrated. In order to establish a number from 0 to 10 to give a trait a rating, the strength of the trait plus the number of times it appears in the writing must be considered to determine an accurate intensity rating. There are also times when a trait has no strength or weakness, it is just there. For example, concentration, desire for responsibility, Greek e's, loyalty, jealousy. In these cases, count is the determining factor.

Don't overlook the other feature: Letters of the alphabet and their traits.
Many beginning G.A.'s have asked me if there was some way to look up a trait by
looking at the letter in which it is found. So, as a result of those requests, I have
done this.

A word of caution to those of you who read this book without the benefit of
schooling from the International Graphoanalysis Society of Chicago, Illinois. While
Graphoanalysis is an accurate tool in personality assessment, a key in putting the
personality together is evaluation: the relationship of traits to one another.
So that a trait that may sound negative in its "raw" state could be softened or
modified by the presence of other traits. For example, in the stable, mature person,
negative traits may lay dormant unless the person is put under extreme stress, and
in the unstable person negative traits may be readily noticed. So use this knowledge
with kindness to yourself and to one another.

Acknowledgements

My thanks to Jackie Thurston, CGA, and Royalynn Lee, MGA, without whose help, ideas and encouragement this book would not have been completed.

Also I wish to thank those people who contributed handwriting samples to help illustrate the traits: Connie Allen, Barbara Bohn, Loyal "Doc" Brush, Virginia Davis, Anita Duncan, Elsie Garrett, Luise Gladden, Esther McNutt, Nan Mize, Betty Rich, Arlene Stranquist, and Leola Wehmeyer; and a special thanks to Lucille Hopkins.

Part One
Dictionary

ACQUISITIVE: (A primary trait)

Initial hook at beginnings of words, or at the beginning of a stroke within a word (does not include circle letters a, o, d, g, q). The size of the hook indicates the size of thing or value desired. Small hooks = desire for small things; large hooks = desire for large possessions or values, such as fame. Major acquisitive (7-10) = grasping.

NO	SMALL	MEDIUM	LARGE	VERY LARGE

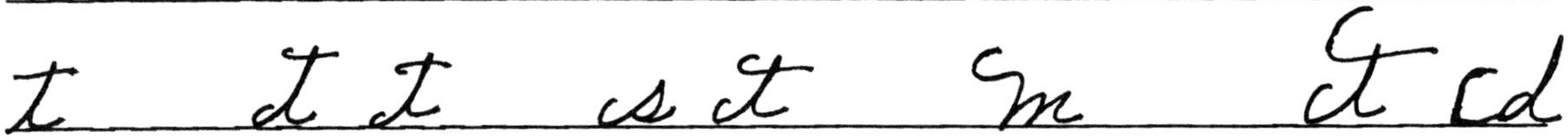

SMALL

MEDIUM

LARGE

VERY LARGE

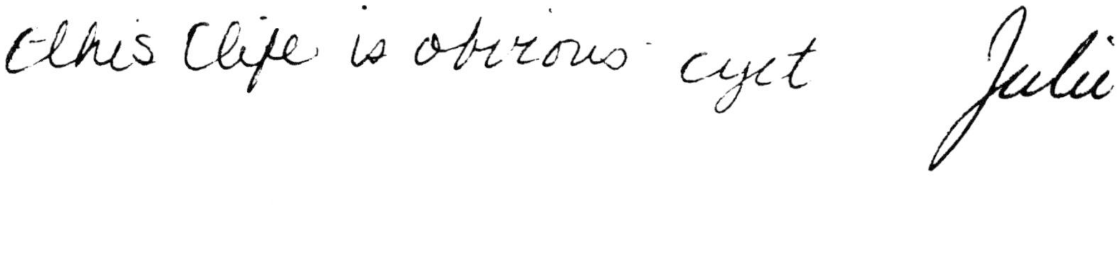

AGGRESSIVE: (A primary trait)

An <u>upstroke</u> that departs <u>obliquely</u> from a <u>downstroke</u> in the same letter <u>below</u> the <u>baseline</u> and <u>drives</u> <u>forward</u>. A break-away stroke below the baseline that moves to the right. Occurs in g's, j's, p's, y's and possibly f's. The longer and stronger the upstroke, the stronger the trait.

NO	WEAK	MODERATE	STRONG
g y j	*g*	*y*	*y*

WEAK

provides greatly good your

MODERATE

good grown-up happy anything

STRONG

wrong together unhappy

AMBITION: (E)

Acquisitive + Self confidence (Large capitals + will power + pride + goals good). The higher the goals and the larger the capitals, the more the ambition. No evaluation of ambition with the independent person.

Intensifiers: Aggressive (minor), analytical, decisive, desire for attention, desire for responsibility, determination, directness, enthusiasm, generosity, imagination material (major), initiative, jealous, persistence, minor sensitiveness, and vanity.

Reductives: Caution, indecisive, pessimism, repression, self conscious, self deceit, self underestimation, shallow, timidity, ultra conservative, weak will power, and yielding.

OPPOSITE: Self underestimation, weak will power, modest.

situation in any event.
Best regards —

Yours truly
Montaldo

Hamilton

ARGUMENTATIVE: (A primary trait)

Found in the lead-in stroke to the small letter "p". To the degree that this stroke rises above the "p" structure is the degree of argumentativeness.

Evaluated: Analytical + impulsive + resentment + sarcasm + stubborn + talkative (all major).

NO (0)   SLIGHT (1-4) _____ (5-7) _____ STRONG (8-10)

0   *Japanese*

1-4   *opportunity*   *puffy*   *position*

5-7   *padded*   *stopped*   *compatible*

8-10   *complete*   *please*   *important*

perpetuating   *Suspicious*   *important*

4

ATTENTION, DESIRE FOR: (A primary trait)

Long, <u>upcurved</u> <u>finals</u> that rise <u>above</u> the <u>mundane</u> letters. If finals turn backward, an excessive amount of attention is desired.

NO (0)	(1-4)	(5-6)	EXCESSIVE (7-10)

consideration)   Conference

1-4   locate.   you   sometimes   sales

5-7   cation problems   towards   you

     Feldman

8-10   then again)   acquire   Riggle

ATTENTION TO DETAILS: (A primary trait)

Closely dotted i's and j's. Supported by well placed punctuation marks.

OPPOSITE: Inattention to details.

In this trait, count is very important, as moderate attention to details or inattention to details are not degrees of attention to details. Either you have it or you don't.

INATTENTION TO DETAILS	MODERATE	ATTENTION TO DETAILS

consider hereditary diseases

Prison is reminds

Seemingly, in delivered

INATTENTION TO DETAILS: (A primary trait)

I-dots far away from the i-stem, or undotted i's or j's.

Supportives: Uncrossed t-stems (unless initiative) and punctuation that is left off.

OPPOSITE: Attention to details:

Attention to details	Mod. atten. to details	Inattention to details

light & mirrors

handwriting beneficial

diversified

ATTENTION SPAN and/or AWARENESS (A primary trait)

(Size of Writing)

Indicated by the height of the mundane area letters (a, c, e, i, m, n, o, p, r, s, u, v, w, x, z).

Concentration (small writing) = mundane letters 1/16" or less

Copybook = mundane letters 2/16"

Large writing = mundane letters 3/16" or larger

BASELINE: (A primary trait)

    Straight baseline = rigid. Intensifies rhythm.
    Slightly bouncey baseline = flexible, versatile.
    Very irregular baseline = unstable; a factor in immaturity.

    Upslant of baseline = optimism.
    Downslant of baseline = pessimism.

STRAIGHT

Licensed in Kansas Jun.

BOUNCEY

Small town in Southeastern Kansas
My earliest memory is of a coll

IRREGULAR

later. To understand how the "hard-warming"
works, this author feels that the focus of attention
be shifted from specific symptoms to the more g
physiological processes underlying those symptom

BLUFF: (A primary trait)

Exceedingly heavy, blunt downstrokes below the baseline. Determination
rates a 10, then comes Bluff. Shown in y's, g's, j's, f's, q's, and p's.

OPPOSITE: Weak or bent determination.

NO   YES

BROADMINDED: (A primary trait)

Broad, well circled e's.

Intensifiers: Moderate, broad and exaggerated philosophical loops, decisive,
fluidity, frankness, generosity, practical goals, humor, loyalty, intuition,
material imagination, analytical/exploratory/investigative thinking, and
moderate to strong will power.

Reductives: Restricted and latent philosophical loops, weak determination,
resistance traits, impulsive, jealousy, narrowminded, selective, self deceit,
superficial thinking, vanity, weak will power and yieldingness.

OPPOSITE: Narrowminded and prejudice.

BROAD   TOLERANT   NARROWMINDED

CAPITALS:

     Size of capitals shows self-esteem or lack of it.

     Twice the height of mundane letters or less = MODEST. (lack self esteem)

     2 1/2 to 3 times the height of mundane letters = SELF ESTEEM.

     If more than 3 times height of mundane = EGOTISTICAL, SUPER EGO.

     If capitals occur within a word or where they shouldn't occur = A DESIRE TO BE IMPORTANT NOT BASED IN REALITY.

MODEST	GOOD SELF ESTEEM	EGOTISTICAL
Pat	*Pat*	*Pat*

MODEST   *So David   phil C.   Amy   Deborah J Alan Stewart,*

GOOD   *Haw Became*

EGO   *Good Regards Bm Enclosed*

CAUTION: (A primary trait)

Long finals at the ends of lines of writing, or lines to fill spaces left
when a sentence ends short of the right-hand margin. Look down the right-
hand margin for caution. Long finals within the writing at the end of
sentences and found consistently, and are not common to other word endings
are also caution.

NO	YES
this trip *can go*	*this trip* — *can go* —

CHANGE, DESIRE FOR: (A primary trait)

    Shown in <u>straight</u> <u>determination</u> strokes in y, g, f, j, and p, which <u>descend</u> at least <u>3 times</u> the height of the mundane letters to begin to qualify for desire for change. The longer the stroke, the stronger the desire for change. Count is important.

    OPPOSITE: Routine.

NO (Routine)	CHANGE	STRONG CHANGE

CHANGE

going to Cambridge University.

sample off to you before certainly

STRONG CHANGE

disputants Company.

Handwriting,

clannish

<u>CLANNISH</u>: (A primary trait)

Small, round or squared <u>circles</u> at the <u>bottom</u> of the <u>determination</u> <u>stroke</u>. Found in j's, g's, y's, p's, z's. The smaller the loop, the stronger the clannishness. If lower loop returns to baseline, it does not qualify for clannishness. Count is important, as is distance from the baseline. Clannish = latent material imagination.

OPPOSITE: Moderate, active, or exaggerated material imagination.

NO (0)	CLANNISH	STRONG CLANNISH

13

COLOR APPRECIATION: (A primary trait)

Color appreciation, depth, and sensuousness are the same trait.

Light (1-4) _____ Mod. (5-6) _____ Mod.Heavy (7-8) _____ Heavy (9-10)

t   *t*   *t*   **t**

1-4   *These pages feel*

5-6   *Ceestines.*
       people   much,

7-8   *position with   successes*
       eventually

9-10   *been making*
       what Conference at Pebble

COMPULSIVE LIAR: (A primary trait)

An "eight" figure combined with an evasive hook on the left side and top of circle letters. A combination of double hook and self deceit. This formation found in "c's" intensifies the trait.

OPPOSITE: Frank.

NO   YES
_____

a d g g   a

chand   acquiring   have   back

drawer   damage

practice

CONCENTRATION: (A primary trait)

Small writing. Indicated when the height of the mundane letters (a, c, e, i, m, n, o, r, s, u, v, w, x, z) measures 1/16" or smaller.

Jackie, I really really felt good about seeing you at the baptismal celebration. Thanks for sharing our joy with me.

The wedding was very beautiful the way turned out. The band w The colors of the wedding were fu wore grey tuxedos, black shoes or light lavender dress with u

and gas for the car out; raise a family on the mo

CONFORMITY: (An evaluated trait)

Pride + dignity + conservative + consistent emotional response.

Intensifiers: Attention to details, cumulative thinking, practical goals, loyalty, organizational ability, persistence, repression, and rhythm.

Reductives: Analytical/exploratory thinking, dominating, independent thinking, self reliance.

yesterday concerned particularly difficult

CONFUSION OF INTERESTS: (A primary trait)

> Writing that overlaps or overruns the writing of the line above. Strokes that conflict with writing in another line of writing. This trait cannot be evaluated if the writing is on lined paper.

NONE	JUST MISSES	MINOR	STRONG

JUST MISSES

discussing *get paid*   *College* *and this*   *Kentucky. Sorry, thank you for*

MINOR

of perfor teracious forward further.   *wage emplo organization convention ce breaking three children*   *fuil a for retiele*

STRONG

my plans me. rely, Dick   *The eq help at very be far a vi and as*   *eupa th fe*

CONSERVATIVE: (A primary trait)

No long spaces between letter formations. Compressed writing.

(Evaluated): Consistent slant, repression, rhythm, and organizational ability.

Reductives: Opposite of traits just listed.

OPPOSITE: Generosity to self.

No Conservative (Generosity to Self)	(5-7) Conservative	(8-10) Conservative
hand	*hand*	*hand*

4

interested in interviewing

5-7

after the death

I would like to have

chance I have to prove to myself & everyone

8-10

altho that would not affect the

most beneficial to

CONSPICUOUS: (An evaluated trait)

Large writing + flourishes.

CONTROLS:

In slant = left-slanted upstrokes (FA) and vertical upstrokes (AB, BC).

In the writing = Conservative, moderate to heavy depth, decisiveness, dignity, directness, good thinking, intuition, pride, rhythm, self confidence, self control, moderate to strong will power.

CREATIVITY: (An evaluated trait)

    1. Material imagination + depth + good thinking = creative thinking.

    2. Material imagination + depth + cumulative + manual dexterity + rhythm + fluidity + intuition = artistic creativity.

OPPOSITE: No imagination.

THINKING

ran my finger into

you men

fishing

ARTISTIC

two please make I owe you & sign? I'd feel

move on to something

CRITICAL: (An evaluated trait)

Major analytical + major exploratory.

NO	YES
man	*MAN*

ana & Nancy day dinner Kennett

courtyard that he would

CULTURE: (An evaluated trait)

Delta "d's", moderate heavy to heavy depth, Greek "e's", Greek "e" in the letter "r", figure 8 formations, fluid g's, intuition, printed capitals.

Intensifiers: Fluidity in f's and in t-bar crossings.

_____ Delta "D"

_____ Greek "E" in letter "e" or "r"

_____ Fluid "F"

_____ Fluid "G", Figure "8" (Literary Leanings)

_____ Intuition

_____ Printed Capitals (Artistic)

_____ Fluidity in T-Bar

DAYDREAMING: (An evaluated trait)

T-bar above the t-stem + weak will power + pride or vanity (t-stem 2 1/2 times or higher than height of mundane letters). If will power is strong, dreams will come true.

NO   YES

to to   *to to*

letter complimenting

DECEIT: (A primary trait)

1. Double loops in small circle formations (a, o, g, q).

2. Combination of double hook and self deceit (compulsive liar) in small circle formations (a, o, g, d, q).

OPPOSITE: Frank.

NO (0)	(1-4)	(5-7)	(8-10)	COMPULSIVE LIAR
o	*O*	*O*	*a*	*a*

1-4   *accounting*

5-7   *stats*

8-10   *growth*

COMPULSIVE LIAR   *addition*

decisiveness

DECISIVENESS: (A primary trait)

   Sturdy, firm, <u>blunt</u> endings. Very strong intensity if there is an increase
   of weight, or a knob is formed at end of stroke. Decisiveness is <u>stronger</u>
   if it appears in the <u>t-bars</u>.

   OPPOSITE: Indecisiveness.

(0)	(1-4)	(5-7)	(8-10)
INDECISIVE	MOD. DECISIVE	DECISIVE	STRONG DECISIVE

5-7   *is a new change move in*

together list F—

8-10   *Arlene lets me than*

23

DEFIANCE: (A primary trait)

1. The buckle of the small letter "k" inflated out of proportion to the rest
    of the mundane writing. The buckle belongs in the mundane area or right
    at the top of the mundane letters. When the buckle invades the abstract
    or philosophical area, the trait of defiance begins and it exists to the
    degree of the exaggeration of the buckle of the letter "k" formation.

2. A large printed "k" (not a capital) out of proportion to the rest of the
    writing.

3. An exaggerated letter within a word (except flat-topped "r"). Not
    seen often.

A little defiance goes a long way. Major defiance = 4 or higher rating.

NO (0)	(1-3)	(4-6)	STRONG (7-10)

1-3   *took   skills   pup   work*

5-6   *knows   like*

7-10   *Bank   skin   know*

<u>DELIBERATE</u>: (A primary trait)

Found primarily in <u>t</u>- and <u>d-stems</u> (sometimes in "l") when the stem is made <u>double</u> (without loops or retracing) Usually has a slightly rounded apex and, as a rule, does not show rigidity.

Secondary evidence can be found in capital M's, N's, or W's, and similar appearing strokes below the baseline. These are only supportive, but do intensify primary indications. Not seen often.

PRIMARY _____ SECONDARY _____

[handwriting samples: "what" (primary), "short" (secondary)]

<u>DEPRESSION</u>: (A primary trait)

Strong pessimism (downslant of lines).

NO _____ YES _____

[handwriting samples: "optimism" (no), "pessimism" (yes)]

[handwriting sample: "analyzed. In the first place I am firm believer in the results of these"]

<u>DEPTH</u>: (A primary trait)

The <u>weight</u> of the writing. Depth, color appreciation, and sensuousness are the same trait.

(1-4) LIGHT	(5-6) MODERATE	(7-8) MOD. HEAVY	(9-10) HEAVY
b	*b*	*b*	*b*

1-4

membered I am taking

job openings

5-6

give their

7-8

there are hourly

the last How

9-10

H Bouvier Tillotson

means. like but much better

DETERMINATION: (A primary trait)

   A <u>straight</u> <u>stroke</u> <u>descending</u> <u>below</u> the <u>baseline</u>. Found in g's, y's, f's, j's.
and can be intensified by downstroke in the letter "p"
The <u>weight</u> equals the amount of force or <u>energy</u> put into <u>finishing</u>. The
weight is determined by the width or heaviness of the stroke as compared to
the weight of the rest of the writing. Remember that downstrokes are usually
heavier than upstrokes.
The <u>length</u> equals the amount of <u>time</u> spent on finishing. The length is
determined by comparing it to the height of the mundane letters.
When the <u>stroke</u> <u>bends</u>, <u>determination</u> <u>stops</u>.

NO (0)	WEAK (1-4)	MODERATE (5-6)	STRONG (7-10)

WEIGHT:

NO

weak

mod.

strong

LENGTH:

short	moderate	long

DIGNITY: (A primary trait)

Retraced t- and d-stems. Intensity is determined by frequency and length of the retracing.

Retraced t-stem = dignified about work.
Retraced d-stem = dignified about style of living or dress.

OPPOSITE: Sensitiveness.

NO   YES
_____

dt dt dt   dt dt dt

utation priest statute toward

sting difficu and   tasks

DIPLOMACY: (A primary trait)

A letter or letters which tapers in size as it proceeds without losing the legibility and identify of the letter or letters involved. Seen in m's, when the last two strokes are progressively lower than the first, but can be seen in any taper involving three (3) strokes.

OPPOSITE: Direct + decisive + frank.

NO   YES
_____

M yes   m yes

miss My Mrs. Olly

seems enjoy mangie pursue

DIRECT: (A primary trait)

Letter formations made <u>without</u> <u>approach</u> <u>strokes</u>, primarily those in which lead-in strokes are considered standard (b, d, f, h, l, t). The following letters made without a lead-in stroke are considered supportive: i, j, m, n, w.

OPPOSITE: Hesitation.

PRIMARY _____ SUPPORTIVE _____

b d f h l t   *i j m n w*

it happens more often in the dorms -

how they will react before

Cap helped me build the system for a small car   *for this*

but love to
shall write to you -   *I have to be*

Man in a job with

<u>DOMINATING</u>:   (An evaluated trait)

1.   Moderate or strong <u>t-bar</u> <u>slanted</u> <u>forward</u> and <u>downward</u>, plus

2.   <u>Decisive</u> or blunt <u>endings</u>.

OPPOSITE: Weak will power or shallowness.

NO   YES
_____

t t   t

secrets this Silence

<u>DOMINEERING</u>:   (An evaluated trait)

1.   <u>Weak</u>, <u>moderate</u> or <u>strong t-bar</u> <u>slanted</u> <u>forward</u> and <u>downward</u> with

2.   <u>Indecisive</u> or feathered <u>endings</u>.

Or: Jealousy + repression + resistance traits + self underestimation.

NO   YES
_____

t t   t

Schneibart   the

EMPATHY: (An evaluated trait)

Slightly looped t- and d-stems + <u>no</u> <u>resistance</u> <u>traits</u>.

culture of personal friendship

deeper depths of each other's life, and one another's helpful

ENTHUSIASM: (An evaluated trait)

T-bar longer than the t-stem is high + moderate or strong will power.

Intensifiers: Aggressive, attention to details, concentration, decisiveness, moderate or heavy depth, determination, dignity, directness, fluidity, material imagination, minor independence, initiative, loyalty, positiveness, pride, rhythm, self confidence, showmanship, sympathy, talkativeness, tenacity, desire for variety, visionary goals, yieldingness.

Reductives: Analytical, conservative, diplomacy, narrowminded, objective, perfectionism, pessimism, poise, reticence, self control, shallowness, weak will power, withdrawal.

OPPOSITE: Precise.

NO _____ YES _____

EVASIVE: (A primary trait)

Initial hook within a circle letter (a, d, g, o, q).

Evaluated: Keen comprehension + deceit + diplomacy + direct.

OPPOSITE: Frank.

NO _____ YES _____

<u>EXAGGERATION</u>: (A primary trait)

Large lower loops. <u>Active</u> or <u>exaggerated</u> <u>material</u> <u>imagination</u>.

<u>Reductives</u>: <u>Analytical</u> thinking, conservative, decisive, <u>dignity</u>, <u>pride</u>, <u>strong</u> <u>will</u> power.

NO	YES

You size appealing projects anyway

saving you enjoy handwriting

<u>EXTRAVAGANCE</u>: (An evaluated trait)

1. Very long endings (<u>extreme</u> <u>generosity</u>) + wide spacing within words (generosity to self or <u>no</u> <u>conservative</u>) + impulsive + yielding + moderate to exaggerated material imagination + possible confusion of interests.

2. Determination + <u>impulsive</u> + <u>indecisive</u> + pride + sensitive + <u>sympathy</u> + yielding + weak will power.

OPPOSITE: Stingy, selfish, or thrifty.

most! We enjoyed each day and have beautiful photos to remind us that

<u>FATALISM</u>:   (A primary trait)

> <u>Drooping</u> <u>of</u> <u>a</u> <u>letter</u> or <u>a</u> <u>single</u> <u>stroke</u>.
>
> 2.   Gentle downward sloping of a line.
>
> The lesser part of fatalism is matter-of-factness.

NO	YES
y h	*y h*

fluidity

FLUIDITY: (A primary trait)

Figure "8's", t-bars flowing into the next letter (th, to, etc.), words that are connected, fluid F's (lower loop reversed).

Secondary indication: Capitals connected to rest of word, or smooth flowing strokes in the writing.

PRIMARY   SECONDARY

to th gave fur   Gave

eight   give me good gliano   gets

time   Though   the

connectedwords

offer   efforts   for Helgbergs

Smoke   Norman   This   Then

office   should   of   shaby

get

35

FORWARD SLANT: (A primary trait)

If _more_ than _half_ the writing is _slanted_ toward the _right_, or leaning toward the right (DE or E+).

NO	YES
Back Vert	Forward

it was the only answer with. So with no sent their wepans up in the room with her, but how was I to know and impact this event would—

FRANK: (A primary trait)

Uncontaminated, _clean_, or plain _circle_ _letters_ (a, d, g, o, and q). Without hooks or loops in circle letters. Can be open (talkative) or closed (reticent).

OPPOSITE: Compulsive liar, deceit, too much evasive or secrecy, or self deceit.

NO	YES
a a a a	a d g o q

properly slip off the sproket. held questions have had of the San Francisco Bay I was invited to resign

GENEROSITY: (A primary trait)

Long finals on words, the width being at least that of the previous letter.
The longer the stroke, the stronger the trait. As soon as the stroke changes
direction, a new trait begins (for example, desire for attention, optimism,
or self castigation).

Secondary indications: Adequate or more than adequate spacing between lines,
words, or in margins. Words are not crowded.

OPPOSITE: Stingy or selfish.

NO _____ YES _____

e h   e h

*Clyde will be more than
look as have
three*

GENEROSITY, EXTREME:

Very long finals on words, the width being more than that of the previous
letter.

Intensifiers: Wide spacing between letters (generosity to self or no
conservative), acquisitive, indecisiveness, and shallowness.

OPPOSITE: Selfish or stingy.

NO _____ YES _____

e h   e h

are   helpful   be

same time self that I give

GENEROSITY TO SELF: (An evaluated trait)

Wide spacing between letters (<u>no conservative</u>) + <u>depth</u> (at least a rating of 5) + <u>no generous endings</u>.

<u>Intensifiers</u>: Broadminded, frank, material imagination, moderate to broad philosophical loops.

<u>Reductives</u>: Caution, conservative, deceit, fears (FA slant, repression, self conscious, timid), restricted philosophical imagination, narrowminded, objective, secrecy, and tenacity.

NO	YES
away	*away*

now running more enjoyable

inadequate To cope with

Some person   Anonymous

Spread out

<u>GOALS</u>: (An evaluated trait)

1. The <u>position</u> of the <u>t-bar crossing</u> on the t-stem in <u>relation</u> to the <u>top</u> of the <u>mundane</u> letters, plus

2. <u>Pride</u> or <u>vanity</u> (t-stem measures a minimum of 2 times or higher than the height of the mundane letters), plus

3. T-bar weight at least the weight of the rest of the writing if writer sets his own goals. If lighter than rest of the writing, will follow the goals of others.

No evaluation of goals is made if t-stem is independent (less than 2 times the height of the mundane letters).

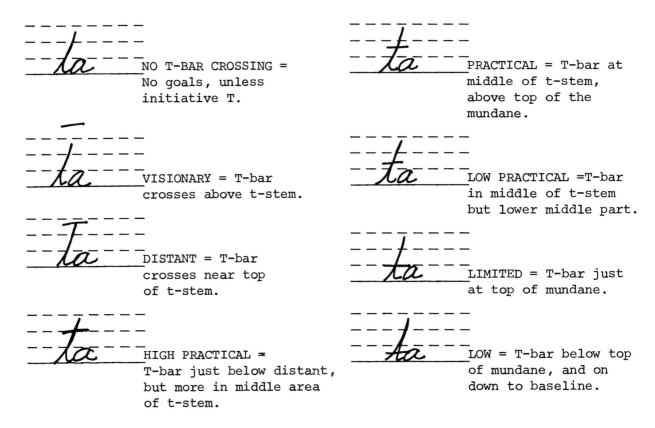

NO T-BAR CROSSING = No goals, unless initiative T.

PRACTICAL = T-bar at middle of t-stem, above top of the mundane.

VISIONARY = T-bar crosses above t-stem.

LOW PRACTICAL =T-bar in middle of t-stem but lower middle part.

DISTANT = T-bar crosses near top of t-stem.

LIMITED = T-bar just at top of mundane.

HIGH PRACTICAL = T-bar just below distant, but more in middle area of t-stem.

LOW = T-bar below top of mundane, and on down to baseline.

NO	VISIONARY	DISTANT	HIGH PRACTICAL	PRACTICAL	LOW PRACTICAL	LIMITED	LOW
ta	ta	ta	ta	ta	ta	ta	ta
to	Th	Salu at	type	ent	ta	to	cistu

HESITATION: (A primary trait)

1. <u>Blobs</u> at the <u>beginning</u> of <u>strokes</u>, or

2. Final downstrokes above the baseline which fade and do not touch the baseline, or

3. I-dots and/or periods which are overdone (retraced over and over).

<u>Supportives</u>: Occasional long spaces between words and long lead-in strokes.

<u>Intensifiers</u>: Conservative, deliberate, fears, superficial thinking, weak will power, and yieldingness.

NO	YES

HUMOR: (A primary trait)

An <u>initial flourish</u> which

1. Begins in the abstract and <u>blends smoothly</u> into the <u>downstroke</u> which reaches the baseline, and

2. Occurs most often in capitals, but can occur in small letters.

Ostentation does not qualify.

NO _____ YES _____

HUMOR, DRY: (A primary trait)

An <u>initial flourish</u> which

1. Begins in the abstract and meets the downstroke at an <u>angle</u>, instead of flowing smoothly into the downstroke.

2. Occurs most often in capitals, but can occur in small letters.

NO _____ YES _____

IDEALISM: (An evaluated trait)

1. Very tall philosophical loops, plus

2. High t-bar crossings, plus

3. Pride or vanity (t's and d's more than 2 times the height of the mundane letters).

NO _____ YES _____

lot   *lot*

the normal complement

father leaving for a year to events

IDIOSYNCRACY (Individualism): (A primary trait)

I-dots made as circles. Also includes periods. Positive when combined with dignity, directness, pride, purpose, and good thinking. Intensifies artistic ability. Negative when combined with ostentation, vanity, and below-average thinking.

NO _____ YES _____

i i   *i o*

im seeing if   *Singin and Ringin*

IMAGINATION, MATERIAL (A primary trait)

    Shown in <u>loops below</u> the <u>baseline</u> in letters g, j, and y. Loop must be made to the <u>left</u> of the <u>downstroke</u> and <u>return</u> to the <u>baseline</u> to qualify. The amount of space inside the loop or the area within the loop as compared to the size of the mundane letters determines the intensity of imagination.

    <u>Intensifiers</u>: Confusion of interests, enthusiasm, generosity, persistence, purpose, responsive, talkative, and keen thinking.

IMAGINATION = a completed loop

LATENT = No loop, or loops that do not return to the baseline (includes aggressive, clannish, and loops made in reverse, to the right of the downstroke).

RESTRICTED = Slender loops, nearly closed (selective).

MODERATE = Width of the loop the same width as the mundane letters.

ACTIVE = Width of loop wider than width of mundane letters (Desire for variety).

EXAGGERATED = Width of loop <u>much</u> wider than width of mundane letters (Strong desire for variety).

(0)	(1-4)	(5-6)	(7-8)	(9-10)
LATENT	RESTRICTED	MODERATE	ACTIVE	EXAGGERATED

LATENT

    recruiting, training, anyway. wrong

    your project any Tough

RESTRICTED   *pay wrong myself. graphs xley*

    your marilyn

MODERATE

See you High myself
pay   you Though you

ACTIVE

you gh agency going Roger

EXAGGERATED

doing you girls jeans

Very good for you. &
that we can be toge

imagination, philosophical

IMAGINATION, PHILOSOPHICAL (An evaluated trait)

Seen in loops above the baseline in L-formations (b, f, h, k, l).

1. Size of loop: The area within the loop or the amount of space within the loop indicates the amount of imagination present:

LATENT = A direct stroke, or a beginning or ending stroke of the loop does not touch the baseline.

RESTRICTED = Very narrow, slender loop, nearly closed.

MODERATE = Loop same width as mundane letters.

BROAD = Loop wider than width of mundane letters. Rounded top intensifies.

EXAGGERATED = Loop much wider than width of mundane letters.

2. The height of the loop indicates the degree of interest:

LESS THAN 2 TIMES the height of the mundane = Philosophy is very practical, not idealistic, and could indicate not using philosophy in life.

2 1/2 to 3 TIMES the height of the mundane = Beginning to use philosophy in everyday life.

3 to 4 TIMES the height of mundane = Philosophical.

4 to 5 TIMES the height of mundane = Very philosophical. Philosophy governs everyday life.

DISTORTED, TWISTED, or WAVINESS in L-structures = Distorted, warped, or twisted philosophy; has received an emotional blow of some sort.

45

LATENT *the from has been*

RESTRICTED *sight each this the*

MODERATE *mutual alert Evelyn*

BROAD *than ship believe really*

EXAGGERATED *awhile loot all*

DISTORTED
WAVINESS *Well yesterday letters bility*

Height of loops:

2 times
  or less *will like Sales follow within Personal*

2 to 3 times *beautiful make learn believe*

3 to 4 times *penmanship the evalua*

4 to 5 times *by however Personnel through* 46

IMMATURE: (A primary trait)

1. <u>Mundane</u> <u>writing</u> = all or most of the letter formations stay within or close to the mundane area.

2. <u>Variable slant</u> = inconsistency or several variations of slant (to the left, straight up, or to the right) and no one area predominates.

<u>Evaluated:</u> Too bouncey baseline + variable slant + weak determination + fears + variable size of letters + weak will power.

1.

> I would like, very much, given the chance to work ... It is a chance to learn

2.

> when you have to think in English and then translate. I had a really good time, even though it was a lot of studying. and I learned a lot. We'll probably go back sometime for the second session but it's $135 a week.

> life work better for me. also become

> better Christian with all this I no I

> will enjoying life to the fullest. beca

IMPATIENCE: (A primary trait)

1. <u>T-bar</u> made to the <u>right</u> of the <u>t-stem</u>, but <u>touching</u>, or

2. Major <u>irritability</u>.

3. Evaluated: Ambition + impulsive + inattention to details + initiative.

Possible causes of: Aggressiveness, desire for change, confusion of interests, domineering, enthusiasm, impulsiveness, desire for variety.

NO	IMPATIENCE
t i	t i

> respect for City

> handwriting sculpture times Divinity

<u>IMPRACTICAL</u>:   (An evaluated trait)

1.   Either all (or <u>most</u>) <u>high</u> <u>t-bar</u> <u>crossings</u>, or all (or <u>most</u>) <u>low t-bar</u> <u>crossings</u>, plus

2.   <u>Pride</u> or <u>vanity</u> (t-stem measures a minimum of 2 times or higher than the height of the mundane letters).

No evaluation of impractical is made with independent t-stems (t-stems less than 2 times the height of the mundane letters).

OPPOSITE: Practical.

NO   IMPRACTICAL

IMPULSIVE: (An evaluated trait)

1. Forward slant (to the right) a minimum of 70%, plus

2. No controls.

Controls: Attention to details, caution, conservative, decisive, moderate
to heavy depth, deliberate, good determination, dignity, diplomacy, left or
vertical slant (FA, AB, BC), no generosity, loyalty, organizational ability,
tall philosophical loops, pride, repression (artificial control), secrecy,
self conscious, self control, good thinking (especially good analytical),
timid, moderate to strong will power, withdrawal.

Intensifiers: Lack of analytical, desire for change, confusion of interests,
daydreaming, light depth, not good determination, direct, enthusiasm,
fluidity, generosity, generosity to self (no conservative), impatience,
inattention to details, indecisive, independent, irritability, keen
comprehension, mundane writing, not well organized, resistance traits
(aggressive, argumentative, defiance, domineering, resentment, sarcasm,
temper), self deceit, sensitive to criticism, superficial thinking, talkative,
desire for variety, weak will power.

Comment: The larger the percentage of forward slant (DE, E+), the greater
the need for controls, otherwise responsiveness turns into impulsiveness.
Barely forward slant (CD) is not a good control.

INATTENTION TO DETAILS: See Attention to Details

INDECISIVE: (A primary trait)

Pointed or feathered-out ending strokes (not firm or blunt). In the T-bar crossing this is the trait of sarcasm (counts as indecisive stroke, though).

Intensifiers: No analytical, argumentative, conservative, deliberate, daydreaming, weak enthusiasm, hesitation, inattention to details, pessimism, procrastination, self conscious, sensitive to criticism, shallow, superficial thinking.

Reductives: Acquisitive, aggressive, attention to details, concentration, desire for responsibility, determination, decisive, direct, enthusiasm, initiative, loyal, objective, optimism, organizational ability, persistence, poise, practical goals, pride, self confidence, self control, tenacity, moderate to strong will, decisive in t-bars is greatest reductive.

Result of: Confusion of interests, weak determination, low goals, latent material imagination, weak will power, yielding.

Concealers: Bluff, conservative, deceit, diplomacy, domineering, stubborn.

OPPOSITE: Decisive.

DECISIVE	MODERATE DECISIVE	INDECISIVE

INDEPENDENT: (A primary trait)

T- and D- stems less than 2 times the height of the mundane letters. Stems can be looped or retraced.

Intensifiers: Acquisitive, aggressive, analytical, argumentative, bluff, clannish, concentration, decisive, defiance, good determination, direct, dominating, domineering, enthusiasm, exaggeration, exploratory, extravagance, frank, idiosyncracy, impulsiveness, initiative, narrowminded, organizational ability, persistence, positive, resentment, selective, self reliance, sarcasm, stubborn, tenacity, moderate to strong will power, withdrawal.

Reductives: Broadminded, caution, conservative, weak determination, dignity, diplomacy, indecisive, jealousy, pride, repression, resistance traits (aggressive, argumentative, defiance, domineering, irritability, resentment sarcasm, stubbornness, temper), self castigation, sensitiveness, sympathy, timid, ultra conservative, vanity, weak will power, yieldingness.

INDEPENDENT	BARE PRIDE	PRIDE	VANITY

INDIFFERENCE: (A primary trait)

Small letters (non-capitals) within a word made larger (out of proportion) than the other small letters. (An exception is the flat-topped "r", the manual dexterity trait; when made larger than the rest of the mundane letters indicates a desire to use the hands in a creative way).

NO   INDIFFERENCE

INDIVIDUALISM: (A primary trait)   See Idiosyncracy

INITIATIVE: (A primary trait)

1. An <u>upstroke</u> that <u>begins</u> at the <u>baseline</u> and <u>breaks away</u> to the <u>right</u> <u>from</u> a <u>downstroke</u>.

2. It is <u>attached</u> to a <u>philosophical loop</u> (h, k,) or to a <u>final</u> t-stem.

The more nearly straight the break-away stroke, the stronger the trait. Length (endurance) and weight (depth or force) are considered. Remember that normally in writing the upstrokes are lighter than the downstrokes, so good initiative can be <u>slightly</u> lighter than the downstrokes.

If the upstroke retraces the preceding downstroke, initiative is not evident. If the break-away stroke is not straight, or the v-formation is not sharp, then initiative is greatly weakened. Analytical thinking is not to be confused with initiative, as initiative must be attached to a stroke that normally comes from the philosophical area.

NO (0)	(1-4)	(5-6)	(7-10)

<u>INSINCERE</u>: (A primary trait)

    Indicated primarily by rating a <u>major</u> in <u>deceit</u>, <u>compulsive liar</u>, <u>shallow</u>, or <u>self deceit</u>.

    <u>Intensifiers</u>: Philosophical loops low (less than 2 times the height of the mundane letters) and irritiability.

    OPPOSITE: Sincere.

DECEIT	COMPULSIVE LIAR	SHALLOW	SELF DECEIT

DECEIT

COMPULSIVE LIAR

SHALLOW

SELF DECEIT

INTEGRITY: (An evaluated trait)

Intensifiers: Major adjustment traits, ambition (self esteem + acquisitive + practical to distant goals + moderate to strong will power), aptitudes (or talent), attention to details, broadminded, caution, conservative, consistent size of letters, depth and slant, upper and lower loops balanced, rhythm, even spacing between letters, words and lines, creativity (moderate to heavy depth + good thinking + material imagination), decisive, moderate to strong determination, dignity, direct, enthusiasm, few or no fears, fluidity, frank, generosity, intuition, loyal, pride (minor independence), few or no resistance or escape traits, self confidence, self control, self reliance, sincere (tall philosophical loops + frank).

Reductives: Major acquisitiveness, weak or no determination, escape traits, (clannish, compulsive liar, concentration, daydreaming, deceit, evasive, procrastination, secretive, self deceit, shallow, superficial thinking, vanity, desire for variety or change), extravagance, fears (desire for attention, indecisive, jealousy, repression, self interest, sensitiveness, stingy, withdrawal), impulsive, major independent, letters that deviate from the norm, narrowminded, perfectionism, prejudice, resistance traits (aggressive, argumentative, defiance, domineering, irritability, resentment, sarcasm, stubbornness, temper), selfish, sensuality, weak will power, yieldingness.

This article touched me tremendously. Then I saw your name. I was not surprised. I am glad you had this experience. I'll see you on the

<u>INTUITION</u>:   (A primary trait)

Breaks <u>between</u> <u>letters</u> in a word.   The more frequent the breaks, the stronger the trait.   Pure printing does not qualify, nor does the break between a capital and the next letter.

(0)	(1-4)	(5-6)	(7-10)

breaks   breaks   breaks   break

1-4   *lovely lady may be among*

5-7   *desire for sucess,*
             act favorably
             for employment.   *further delay the*
                                        into the heaven

8-10   *things regarding regular*

<u>INVENTIVE</u>:   (An evaluated trait)

1.   Analytical/investigative/cumulative thinking, plus

2.   No material imagination.

Can come up with an invention, but doesn't get along well with others...doesn't have imagination in solving people problems.

IRRITABILITY: (A primary trait)

Distorted i-dots made with a <u>jab</u> or irregular <u>short</u> <u>dashes</u>. (Not a round or circle i-dot).   The larger and heavier the jabs, the stronger the irritability. Can be irritability to self_____ <i>i</i> _____, others _____ <i>ī</i> _____, or just plain irritability_____ <i>i</i> _____.

OPPOSITE: Loyalty (patience).

(0)	(1-4)	(5-7)	(8-10)

ISOLATING TRAITS:

Escape traits (clannish, compulsive liar, concentration, daydreaming, deceit, evasive, procrastination, secretive, self deceit, shallow, superficial think-ing, vanity, desire for variety), resistance traits (aggressive, argumenta-tive, defiance, domineering, irritability, resentment, sarcasm, stubbornness, temper), and withdrawal.

jealousy

JEALOUSY: (A primary trait)

A <u>small</u> <u>inverted</u> <u>initial</u> <u>loop</u> that:

1. Is <u>attached</u> to a <u>downstroke</u> or could be on a <u>t-bar</u>.

2. <u>Starts</u> with a "<u>back-to-self</u>" stroke.

3. Usually occurs in capital letters, but can appear on any letter.

The smaller the loop, the stronger the jealousy.

<u>Intensifiers</u>: Acquisitive, depth, desire to attention, domineering, egotism, imagination (material), impulsive, irritability, narrowminded, prejudice, resentment, self conscious, self deceit, selfish, stubborn, tenacity, vanity.

<u>Reductives</u>: Analytical, broadminded, exploratory, fluidity, generous, intuition, objective, self confident, self reliant, sympathy, yielding.

<u>Symptoms</u>: Aggressive, clannish, desire to attention, domineering, indecisive, selective, self interest, self underestimation, selfish, sensitiveness, timid, vanity.

<u>Concealers</u>: Deceit, dignity, diplomacy, poise, pride, repression, reticent, secrecy.

NO   JEALOUSY

LARGE WRITING: (A primary trait)

Height of the <u>mundane</u> section of writing (a, c, e, i, m, n, o, r, s, u, v, w, x,) <u>measures</u> <u>3/16"</u> or <u>higher</u>.

leadership

LEADERSHIP: (An evaluated trait)

Analytical thinking, copybook size writing (no concentration), creativity,
decisive, determination, enthusiasm, exploratory thinking, frank, initiative,
pride (minor independence), slant forward, moderate to strong will power.

Intensifiers: Acquisitive, aggressive (minor), broadminded, diplomacy,
direct, fluidity, generous, intuition, loyal, optimism, persistence,
tall philosophical loops, and positive.

Reductives: Concentration, deceit, weak or short determination, no
exploratory or analytical thinking, low goals, latent material imagination,
indecisive, independent (major), narrowminded, resentment, sarcasm, self
deceit, back or vertical slant, vanity, weak will power.

Dear Lorraine –

Your expertise may get

To: JTC

Interesting + selection.

I suggest you consider tennis + golf books next time; possibly

LINE APPRECIATION: (An evaluated trait)

1. Gracefully-made lower loops.

2. And graceful-looking capitals.

3. And straight, printed structures, or added straight lines to cross downstrokes.

4. Balance between structures above and below the baseline.

5. Rhythm.

6. Artistic ability.

1. *just   you a gain*

2. *The Florida Chapter   Connie*

3. *Daily They Hamilton Brent*

LOYALTY: (A primary trait)

Round i- and j-dots and periods. The lighter the dot, the stronger the loyalty.

NO	STRONG IRRITABLE	MODERATE IRRITABLE	MODERATE LOYALTY	STRONG LOYALTY
i i	*i*	*i*	*i*	*i*

handwriting analysists in publicity

invitation stantially in- in

<u>MANUAL DEXTERITY</u>:   (An evaluated trait)

1. Any <u>flat-topped</u> structure found in the mundane area of writing.
   Could be a squared, flat-topped letter "r", or flat-topped m's or n's,
   or could be a straight line, horizontal to the baseline connecting two
   letters (many times seen between the letter "o" and the following letter).
   If the flat-topped structure rises above the rest of the mundane letters,
   the trait is intensified.....the writer has a "need" to use hands or feet.

2. Plus cumulative thinking.

If there is no cumulative thinking in the writing, then writer can use hands
and feet as an added dimension to the personality, but there is no "need"
or talent for manual dexterity.

NO	MANUAL DEXTERITY	RISES ABOVE MUNDANE
✗	M.WOO	large

was front one basis phone

some someone   I worked for
approximately two

a nice future and
to improve myself.

MATTER-OF-FACTNESS: (A primary trait)

Finals that have a prolonged down-slant.

NO	MATTER-OF-FACT
e	*e*

none   inspection   upon   maine

machine advance   matter of fact

farmed and they had

modest

MODEST: (A primary trait)

Lack of good self confidence. <u>Capital</u> letters made <u>twice</u> or <u>less</u> the <u>height</u> of the <u>mundane</u> area letters.

NO	MODEST
Henry	*Henry*

Wednesday, May 20, 1981. Today

also I feel that Marilyn   *Mary Helen*

*I have **In all my years** God in*

MUNDANE WRITING: (A primary trait)

All or most of the letter formations stay within or close to the mundane area of writing (a, c, e, i, m, n, o, r, s, u, v, w, x).

NO	MUNDANE WRITING

the   *the*

Thank-you   Each such conflict

sleep from   hillsides in a

of steaming   water which

it, I wouldn't even attempt to try it.

so we won't go until summer or fall. I'm in no hurry though. I'm not planning on going to France until I've graduated.

NARROWMINDED: (A primary trait)

Narrow "e's". Intensified by narrow or latent philosophical loops.

Reduced by moderate, broad, or exaggerated philosophical loops.

VERY BROAD	BROADMINDED	TOLERANT	NARROWMINDED
l	*l*	*l*	*ll*

These are   I became the   please

We remove the blower student

OBJECTIVE: (A primary trait)

Vertical (AB) section of the slant. The percentage of vertical slant (AB) =
the degree of the trait. For example of AB = 30, the trait intensity is 3.
If AB = 50, then trait intensity is 5. BC slant intensifies.

Reductives: Lack of good analytical, desire for attention, strong fears,
repression, lack of rhythm, strong secrecy, self conscious, slant forward,
stingy.

OPPOSITE: Impulsive.

NO _____ OBJECTIVE _____

Back _forward_ _Verticle_

Symphony Finance Committee, because I

Thank you for the comments

for the Office, he asked one of the

OPTIMISM: (A primary trait)

Shown primarily in the general <u>upward</u> <u>slant</u> of <u>lines</u> of writing. Secondary indications: upward slanted words, letters, or t-bars, or upturned finals on words. To the degree that the lines go up = trait intensity. Optimism <u>cannot</u> be <u>evaluated</u> if writing is on <u>lined</u> <u>paper</u>.

OPPOSITE: Pessimism.

NO	OPTIMISM
lines go down	*lines go up*

a opportunity to buy
but a "Florida" house —

associates excluded

ORGANIZATIONAL ABILITY: (A primary trait)

Shown in the letter "f" when the upper and lower portions of the stem are balanced, or equal distance from the baseline.
If no loops, but balanced = can get self organized.
If has upper and lower loops and balanced = can get self and others organized.

Evaluated: Can be evaluated from balance of upper and lower loops (other than "f") in the rest of the writing.

(0)	(1-4) (just misses)	(5-7)	(8-10)

1-4   *family factor funding*

5-7   *for refuse first.*

8-10   *difference for*

OSTENTATION: (A primary trait)

Unnecessary, excessive, tasteless ornamentation. Usually found in capitals and signatures, but can be seen elsewhere. Not pleasing to the eye.

OPPOSITE: Showmanship or printed capitals.

NO	OSTENTATION

PATCHING: (A primary trait)

Writer goes <u>back</u> <u>over</u> <u>writing</u> and <u>corrects</u> any <u>missing</u> <u>strokes</u>, or <u>miss-</u>
<u>spelled</u> <u>words</u>, or <u>strokes</u> <u>made</u> <u>in</u> <u>error</u>. If writer uses pencil, erasing may
be the method used to correct mistakes.

1. Patching combined with good thinking = perfectionism.

2. Patching combined with poor thinking = inept effort to patch up a
poorly done job, just doing a sloppy job.

NO	PATCHING
He goes to town	*He's to town*

1.

job ate the hospital ?
in the pediatricks (SP)
, now . . .

2.

and he
get you
it all
you me
month
to came
Early,

Early
I was quite interesting
by the interests and oppo
Each year, as then were
similarities and differen
at a comparable age.

PERFECTIONISM: (An evaluated trait)

    1. Attention to details + dignity + carefully written, legible letters + even size of letters + loyal + even margins + organizational ability + precision + rhythm + consistent slant + even spacing.

    2. Or, patching + good thinking.

1.

issue. The lyrics of this song composed by a very gifted indi named Jim Croce who has since to that heavenly dimension in the song is still an original but by not I. What an embarrassment - that Mr. Croce produced this w

2.

grandmother + m
ticular. In the
Tell Rusty
lonely knew ''

PERSISTENCE: (A primary trait)

A <u>tie-formation</u> consisting of:

1. An <u>upstroke</u> that <u>departs</u> from a <u>downstroke</u>, <u>either</u> to the <u>right</u> or to the
    <u>left</u>.

2. The upstroke then moves to the <u>left</u>.

3. <u>Forms</u> a <u>loop</u> as it returns in a <u>downward</u> <u>swing</u>.

4. <u>Crosses</u> <u>itself</u> and the <u>downstroke</u> from which it started.

OPPOSITE: Weak determination.

NO   PERSISTENCE

PESSIMISM: (A primary trait)

Primarily shown in <u>down-slanted</u> <u>lines</u> of writing. <u>Cannot</u> be <u>evaluated</u> when writing is done on <u>lined</u> <u>paper</u>.

Extreme pessimism = when the whole writing has a downhill appearance.

<u>Intensifiers</u>: Down-slanted words and ending strokes.

OPPOSITE: Optimism.

NO   PESSIMISM

optimism

Pessimism

*in the other place. I
always said that nobody aas*

PHYSICALMINDED: (A primary trait)

Found in the <u>lower</u> <u>loop</u> of the <u>small</u> <u>letter</u> "<u>p</u>". The <u>size</u> of the <u>loop</u> plus the frequency indicates the degree of intensity.

(0) Precise	(1-4)	(5-7)	(8-10)
p	*p*	*p*	*p*

1-4   *up dap exceptions*

5-7   *persons*

8-10 *Companion Potential*

POISE: (A primary trait)

    <u>Vertical</u> slanted writing (AB).

    Evaluated: <u>Forward slant</u> (DE, E+) + <u>controls</u>. Controls in the slant =
left or vertical slant (FA, AB, BC). Controls in the writing = conservative,
decisive, moderate to heavy depth, determination, dignity, direct, intuition,
pride, rhythm, self confidence, self control, good thinking, moderate to
strong will power.

    OPPOSITE: Impulsive.

I'll work on this —

five months since the accident
our 2+ monthold son, Ivan.

The Florida Chapter has

contact with

POSITIVE: (A primary trait)

A <u>downstroke</u> descending <u>straight</u> to the <u>baseline</u> from the <u>philosophical</u> <u>area</u>.
Shown in t's, L-structures (b's, f's, h's, k's, l's), and capitals.

Remember that downstrokes are usually heavier than upstrokes, so positive
stroke will look as heavy or heavier than the rest of the writing to qualify.
Positive is not often seen in writing as a major trait.

NO _____ POSITIVE _____

PRACTICAL: (An evaluated trait)

<u>All</u> or <u>most</u> <u>t-bar</u> <u>crossings</u> in the <u>practical</u> area of <u>t-stem</u>, plus pride or
vanity.

NO _____ PRACTICAL _____

PRECISE: (An evaluated trait)

1. Retraced stem in lower loop of small letter "p",

2. Plus short, balanced t-bars (the shorter the t-bar, the more precise),

3. Plus attention to details.

Intensifiers: Carefully made letters, concentration, conservative, dignity, pride, rhythm.

NO	PRECISE
p t i	*p t i*

page paper drop,

testing. continent, Contact

PREJUDICE: (An evaluated trait)

Narrowminded + moderate to heavy depth + forward slant (DE, E+).

Intensifiers: Restricted or latent philosophical imagination loops.

NO	PREJUDICE
need	*need*

An equity interest

but when I get ready,

waste time and money

It seems easier not to

PRIDE: (A primary trait)

T- and D- stems that measure from 2 to 2 3/4 times the height of the mundane area of writing. Stems may be retraced or looped.

Bare pride = 2 times the height of the mundane.

Pride = between 2 and 2 3/4 times the height of the mundane area letters.

Pride in t-stems = pride in work done (use under forces to achieve)

Pride in d-stems = pride in dress, lifestyle, decisions made.

NO PRIDE	BARE PRIDE	PRIDE
to d to d	to d	to d

Bare
Pride   *standing parents hard at experienced*

Pride   *etc. but going to to do*

PROCRASTINATION: (A primary trait)

T-bars made to the left of the t-stem.

Supportive: I-dots or j-dots made to the left of i- or j-stem (procrastination in little things).

OPPOSITE: Impatience.

NO	PROCRASTINATION
t t i	t t i

Cathy industry negative in the

76

PURPOSE: (An evaluated trait)

Minimum practical goals (maximum distant) + good determination + pride or vanity + moderate to strong will power.

OPPOSITE: Weak will power or limited or low goals.

NO	PURPOSE
toy	*toy*

chats. Thanks for

came at a time

Thank you for your interesting letter

of that type of team

efforts and their contributions
one of us wants

(turn to page reference?)

REJECTION: (A primary trait) (Feels rejected)

Shown in a reversed lower loop in y, j, g.

NO	REJECTION

my   family

REPRESSION: (A primary trait)

The upward retracing of a downstroke above the baseline. Found primarily
in the mundane area but may extend into the philosophical area.   Shown
in m's, n's, h's, k's, r's.   The farther up the retracing, the stronger the
trait.

(0)	(1-4)	(5-7)	(8-10)

1-4   _while beyond John_

5-7   _The economic gulf that has_

8-10   _remember   J am applying for the job_

J'm sending a stamp so it can be

resentment

RESENTMENT: (A primary trait)

Straight initial upstroke that begins at or below the baseline, goes up to connect with another stroke. Stronger when such a lead-in stroke is not usually found at the beginning of that letter. If the initial upstroke bends there is no resentment. The longer the stroke below the baseline = comes from the past; length of stroke below baseline determines from how far into the past it has come. Weight of stroke intensifies.

Intensifiers: Attention to details, confusion of interests, depth, domineering, exaggeration, exploratory-analytical thinking, generosity, material imagination, impulsive, independent, loyal, narrowminded, ostentation, perfectionism, persistence, pessimism, repression, sensitiveness, moderate or strong will power, tenacity, vanity.

Reductives: Broadminded, caution, direct, no generosity, keen thinking, intuition, objective, self control, self interest, shallow.

Signals: Aggressive, defiance, irritability, jealous, sarcasm, stubborn, suspicion, temper.

Concealers: Deceit, dignity, diplomacy, poise, pride, reticent, secrecy, self conscious, timid.

NO _____ RESENTMENT _____

_____ *a* _____ */a* _____

is a very their want lower to

to get financial) in on rigas

79

RESPONSIBILITY, DESIRE FOR: (A primary trait)

Large, inverted initial loop on a stroke that returns to the baseline and starts with a "back-to-self" stroke. It may be seen on a t-bar. The larger the loop, the more the desire.

Evaluated: Attention to details + creativity (imagination + good thinking) + decisive + determination + direct + practical goals + initiative + organizational ability + pride + moderate to strong will power.

Intensifiers: Acquisitive, aggressive, determination, enthusiasm, persistence, positive, tenacity.

NO	DESIRE FOR RESPONSIBILITY
m	*m*

RESPONSIBILITY, WISH FOR   (A primary trait)

Large initial hook on a stroke that returns to the baseline. It may be seen on a T-bar.

NO	YES
m	*m*

RESPONSIVE: (An evaluated trait)

Major forward slant (DE, E+) + controls in slant (left slanted or vertical, FA, AB, BC) and/or controls in the writing.

Controls: Analytical, caution, conservative, cumulative, clannish, decisive, dignity, diplomacy, good thinking, narrowminded, organizational ability, poise, pride, repression, reticence, rhythm, secretive, selective, self conscious, self control, sensitiveness to criticism, timid, moderate to strong will power, withdrawal.

that I needed a good word.

Irene, but it's been making

Things up here are moving along.

sure of the crack. Then we have a

RESTLESS: (An evaluated trait)

Desire for <u>variety</u> + desire for <u>physical</u> activity.

<u>Controls</u>: Analytical, attention to details, caution, conservative, cumulative thinking, decisive, deliberate, good thinking, narrowminded, organizational ability, perfection, precise, poise, pride, repression, rhythm, selective, self conscious, self control, selective, timid, moderate to strong will power, withdrawal.

NO	RESTLESS
party	*Party*

improving each has been "dangling"   *Stay healthy stay happy*

RETICENCE: (An evaluated trait)

<u>Closed</u> <u>circle</u> <u>letters</u> (a, d, g, o, q). Intensified by <u>narrow</u> <u>circle</u> <u>letters</u> and <u>latent</u> <u>material</u> <u>imagination</u>.

If reticence is 100% by count, but circle letters are round and full (imagination in the area of conversation) = will talk.

If reticence = 100% + round circle letters + forward slant + imagination = will talk.

(0)	(1-4)	(5-7)	(8-10)
a	*a o*	*a o*	*a o*

about a group   *can report*   *and water*

information

RHYTHM: (An evaluated trait)

Even returning of downstrokes to the baseline + even baseline.

Evaluated: Even baseline + even size of small letters + even size of
capitals + consistent slant + even returning of strokes to baseline + even
spacing between words, lines and letters.

Rhythm intensifies depth, imagination, intuition, literary ability, musical
talent, manual dexterity, organizational ability, physicalmindedness, and
good thinking.

It seems Sue really had some strange experiences
has been in & out of the hospital since Nov 30th _ intense
whole bit. Was just miserable in the nursing home so.

to work up with
next season's t
continue from Oc
a bad season eh?

And Challenge
interested in w
for this posit

ROUTINE: (A primary trait)

Determination stroke (below baseline) that measures less than 2 times the
height of the mundane area letters.

NO   ROUTINE

years   *my*   *WRONG*   *My years*

for the job of testing for
have been working for

SARCASM: (A primary trait)

T-bar made with indecisive or needle-pointed ending.

NO	SARCASM
t	*t*

but *get* *suggest* *to the*

tennis *lot*

SECRECY: (A primary trait)

Loop on right side of circle formation (a, g, o, q).

Size of loop + count = intensity.

(0)	(1-4)	(5-7)	(8-10)
O	*O*	*O*	*O* *O*

1-4   *for*   *another*   *company*

5-7   *discouraging*

8-10   *bombing*   *mouths*

of people.
problems   *complete*

selective

SELECTIVE: (A primary trait)

Slender or narrow lower loop in which the upstroke is brought up to or through the baseline. Restricted material imagination. Lies between moderate and retraced lower loops.

NO	SELECTIVE

q y ----------------- *g y* -------------

myself. why lawyers gives college

SELF CASTIGATION: (A primary trait)

A stroke that swings upward and backward over the preceding letters to cross a t-stem.

2. Or t-bar crossings made from right to left.

Intensifiers: Defiance, jealousy, narrowminded, pessimism, resentment, vanity.

NO	SELF CASTIGATION

to   *get*

the   *night tablet*   *alot but*   *two*

night

85

SELF CONFIDENT: (An evaluated trait)

Capitals at least 2 1/2 times the height of mundane + minimum practical goals + moderate to strong will power + pride or vanity.

The higher the goals and the larger the capitals, the stronger the trait.

NO   SELF CONFIDENT
_____

Betty   *Betty*
_____

Here's   *Marge Huxtable*
first.

SELF CONSCIOUS: (A primary trait)

Final hump of m or n that rises above the rest of the letter, or when the second letter of double letters is higher than the first.   The higher the last stroke, the stronger the self consciousness.   Check to find the highest hump in the writing to determine intensity under pressure.

(0)	(1-4)	(5-7)	(8-10)
m	m	m	m

1-4   *been and is   may   added*

5-7   *Mr. Farley   more   Burkett*

8-10   *May all your*
       fall into place

SELF CONTROL: (A primary trait)

    Shown in <u>t-bar</u> <u>crossings</u> that <u>bend</u> so that <u>ends</u> <u>turn</u> <u>downward</u>.

NO	SELF CONTROL

t t   *t*

the expect moment. But both

SELF DECEIT: (A primary trait)

    <u>Initial</u> <u>loop</u> <u>inside</u> <u>circle</u> <u>letter</u> (a, d, g, o, q). An "e" structure on the <u>left</u> side of the <u>circle</u> letter. The larger the loop, the stronger the trait.

(0)	(1-4)	(5-7)	(8-10)
a	*a*	*a*	*a*

1-4   *law Colorado early*

5-7   *jeans that What*

8-10   *realiz ology. predict places*

87

SELF ESTEEM: (A primary trait)

>   Shown in <u>large</u> <u>capitals</u>, a <u>minimum</u> of <u>2 1/2</u> <u>times</u> the <u>height</u> of the mundane
>   letters.
>
>   OPPOSITE: Modest (small capitals, less than 2 times height of mundane
>   letters).

(0)	(5-7)	(8-10)
Henry	*Henry*	*Henry*

5-7   *States*   *Bob on "Perspectives"?*

8-10   *Helzbergs.*   *Sam & Louie*   *Anne*

SELF RELIANCE: (A primary trait)

>   <u>Underscore</u> of a <u>signature</u>.

Betty Ric   *Love Harold*   *Montaldo*

Sincerely,   *Glendale Rider*

Harriet Guthrie

<u>SELF UNDERESTIMATION</u>: (An evaluated trait)

<u>T-bar</u> <u>crossings</u> placed <u>low</u> on the <u>t-stem</u> (at the top of the mundane letters or lower) + <u>pride</u> or <u>vanity</u>. Trait becomes stronger as the t-bar gets closer to the baseline. No evaluation of self underestimation is made if the writing is independent thinking.

OPPOSITE: Ambition.

(0)	(5-7)	(8-10)

t   *to*   *to*

to contribute built interesting

must admit to first time

SELFISH: (An evaluated trait)

1. No generosity + vertical (AB) slant + conservative.

2. No generosity + acquisitive + generosity to self + tenacity.

3. No generosity + acquisitive + moderate to heavy depth + tenacity.

4. No generosity + left slant (FA) + possible tenacity.

SENSITIVENESS TO CRITICISM: (An evaluated trait)

1. Looped t- and d- stems + pride, or

2. Impulsive + resentment.

Intensifiers: Attention to details, concentration, depth, diplomacy, material imagination, impulsive, indecisive, individualism, jealousy, narrow-minded, perfection, prejudice, resentment, self castigation, self conscious, self deceit, self underestimation, forward slant, suspicion, tenacity, timid.

Reductives: Broadminded, conservative, defiance, dignity, latent material imagination, independent, objective, vanity.

Symptoms: Clannish, daydreaming, domineering, impatience, irritability, procrastination, sarcasm, selective, stubborn, temper.

Concealers: Bluff, deceit, diplomacy, objective, poise, repression, reticence, secrecy, self confidence, withdrawal.

OPPOSITE: Dignity.

(0)	(1-4)	(5-7)	(8-10)
_dt_	_dt_	_dt_	_dt_

1-4   _do something_

5-7   _to field end_

8-10   _head don't understand and desperately to position action._

SENSUOUSNESS: (A primary trait)

The <u>weight</u> of the writing. Depth and color appreciation are the same trait.
<u>Clean</u> <u>strokes</u>, no blobs, no inked-in letters, no corrugations, no waviness
or shakiness.

(1-3) LIGHT DEPTH	(4-5) MOD. DEPTH	(6-7) MOD. HEAVY DEPTH	(8-10) HEAVY DEPTH
ℓ	ℓ	ℓ	$\boldsymbol{\ell}$

1-4   *November 5, 1975*   *same as at*
                                          sleep which is

5-6   *none exists.*   *my constant*
             and use

7-8   *Number five*   *Personal friend*
                what types of
      and sincere   *would be able.*
          We do

9-10   *ref — granola*   *together.*
      yogurt — olive
    peanut oil & all

SHAKINESS (OR WAVINESS): (A primary trait)

Strokes in the writing appear to be shaky, wavy, wobbly, jerky, uneven.

NO	SHAKINESS
ℓ g	ℓ g

Dave believe Grandview restrain

and I am too self conscious of across
this all had a lot to
I drank so much..

SHALLOWNESS: (A primary trait)

Curved t-bar crossings that are higher at the ends than in the middle. Basin-shaped t-bars. Exceptions are when a persistence stroke is part of the t-bar crossing, and when fluidity is part of the t-bar crossing. A rating of 4 or higher makes this a major trait.

(0)	(1-4)	(5-7)	(8-10)
t t	t	t	t

1-4   *situa into effect*

5-7   *light starting most*

8-10   *writing cut.*

SHOWMANSHIP: (A primary trait)

    Tasteful embellishment or ornamentation of capitals, pleasing to the eye.

    Evaluated: Moderate to heavy depth + flourishes well made in capital letters + material imagination + intuition + line value + rhythm.

NO	SHOWMANSHIP
M	*m*

SINCERE: (An evaluated trait)

    Frank + tall philosophical loops + loyal.

This article touched me tremendously. Then I saw your name. I was not surprised. I am glad you had

system before one attempts to monitor and fee before one attempts to monitor and feedback

SLANT: (A primary trait)

    Indicated by the <u>slant</u> of the <u>upstrokes</u> of the writing.

    Back slant (slant toward left or FA) = when <u>more</u> than <u>1/2</u> the <u>upstrokes</u> in the writing <u>slant</u> toward the <u>left</u> or lean toward the left.

(handwriting sample: "influence been fantastic for her well as our relationship.")

    Vertical (AB, BC) = When <u>more</u> than <u>1/2</u> the <u>upstrokes</u> appear to go <u>straight up</u>.

(handwriting sample: "to the heart of London the future and with absolutely what his new existance encor")

    Forward (CD, DE, E+) = When <u>more</u> than <u>1/2</u> the <u>upstrokes</u> in the writing appear to be <u>slanted</u> or leaning toward the <u>right</u>.

(handwriting sample: "relate well to people I welcome responsibility If you are")

STINGY: (an evaluated trait)

1. No generosity + acquisitive + conservative + tenacity.

2. No generosity + conservative + no wide spacing between words.

3. No generosity + possible acquisitive + repression + self interest (FA)
    + ultra conservative.

Intensifiers: Acquisitive, caution, concentration, confusion of interests,
decisive, heavy depth, attention to details, independence, jealousy, loyal,
narrowminded, perfectionism, pessimism, positive, repression, restricted
philosophical loops, reticence, self castigation, self conscious, self
deceit, self underestimation, selfish, shallow, FA slant, tenacity, timid,
vanity, strong will power, withdrawal.

Reductives: Aggressive, broadminded, light depth, generosity, moderate
material imagination, impulsive, indecisive, optimism, pride, self
confidence, self reliance, sensitiveness, sympathy, yielding, weak will power.

Signals: No analytical, no exploratory, no generosity, latent or restricted
material imagination, repression.

Concealers: Deceit, dignity, diplomacy, poise, pride, secrecy.

You may be wondering why (?) I am writing
appreciation, & thanks at this time... it would be
allow me to explain. I've had the good fortune to
ted approval for a transfer to the honor farm, gi
custody, & the added approval for a work release

When love beckons to you follow.
Though his ways are hard & steep.
And when his wings enfold you yu
Though his voice may shatter yo

STUBBORN: (A primary trait)

A wedge, or inverted "v", usually seen in t- and d-stems, in which the upstroke need not be straight, but the downstroke is usually very straight. The wider the wedge, and the straighter and heavier the strokes, the stronger the intensity of the trait.

(0)	(1-4)	(5-7)	(8-10)
t d	t	d	A

1-4   writing dull and the

5-7   patient art

8-10   the here there

short the

SYMPATHY: (An evaluated trait)

Broadminded, generous, humor, material imagination, intuition, pride, loyalty, slight sensitiveness (empathy), forward slant.

Reductives: Fears (desire for attention, indecisive, jealousy, repression, self-castigation, self-consciousness, self-underestimation, sensitiveness, stingy, timid, ultra conservative, withdrawal) and resistance traits (aggressive, argumentative, defiance, domineering, irritability, resentment, sarcasm, stubborn, temper).

always fathoming, with newer n e deeper dep the of each other's life, and richer veins of one another's help ful

<u>TALKATIVE</u>:   (A primary trait)

    <u>Circle</u> <u>letters</u> (a, d, g, o, q) that are <u>not</u> <u>closed</u>. Varies from hardly visible to a wide gap.

    Evaluated: <u>Round</u> <u>circle</u> <u>letters</u> + <u>material</u> <u>imagination</u> + <u>reticence</u> + <u>forward</u> <u>slant</u>.

        (or)   Squeezed or narrow circle letters + talkative + latent or restricted material imagination = talks about very limited subjects, such as only work, or only children, or only spouse, etc.

    <u>Intensifiers</u>:   Roundedness of <u>circle</u> <u>letters</u>, enthusiasm, <u>material</u> <u>imagination</u>, <u>resentment</u>, <u>forward</u> <u>slant</u>.

    <u>Reductives</u>:   Cramped or narrow circle letters, major left or vertical slant (FA or AB), latent or restricted material imagination, timid, ultra conservative.

    OPPOSITE: Reticence.

(0)	(1-4)	(5-7)	(8-10)
a	*a*	*a*	*u*

1-4   *Thought please*

5-7   *you. nearly south*

8-10   *into latest*

<u>TEMPER</u>: (A primary trait)

1. <u>T-bars</u> made to the <u>right</u> of the <u>t-stem</u>, not touching or crossing. Light t-bar = weak annoyance; short heavy t-bar = explosive temper.

2. A <u>tic</u> at the <u>beginning</u> of a <u>stroke</u>. It is a short, straight, inflexible stroke, neither grounded nor braced. The shorter and heavier the tic, the more the temper.

<u>Intensifiers</u>: Major analytical, enthusiasm, no generosity, impulsive, irritability, physicalminded, resistance traits (aggressive, argumentative, defiance, domineering, resentment, sarcasm, stubborn, temper), sensitiveness, forward slant, talkative.

<u>Reductives</u>: (AB) vertical slant, dignity, diplomacy caution, generosity, humor, left slant (FA), pride, reticence, good thinking, self control, self consciousness, ultra conservative.

NO	TEMPER
t	*t*

At the certainly treatment. St.

<u>TENACITY</u>: (A primary trait)

<u>Final</u> <u>hook</u> on a stroke. Primarily at the end of a word. Within the word intensifies.

(0)	(1-4)	(5-7)	(8-10)
t y	*t y*	*t y*	*t y*

1-4 To! how debts ring.

5-7 felt tips, paid

8-10 base and live surface.

THINKING (MENTAL) PROCESSES: (A primary trait)

Shown primarily in m's, n's, h's, but can be seen in other strokes in the mundane area.   There are 6 thinking processes:

1.   Analytical = v-formations.
2.   Cumulative = rounded strokes.
3.   Exploratory = inverted "v".
4.   Investigative = falls between cumulative and exploratory.   Inverted "v" with slightly rounded apex.   Could be low exploratory or exploratory with a slightly rounded apex, or apexes that are not good and sharp.
5.   Keen comprehension = needle-pointed strokes.
6.   Superficial = strokes that stay close to the baseline and are ill-formed.

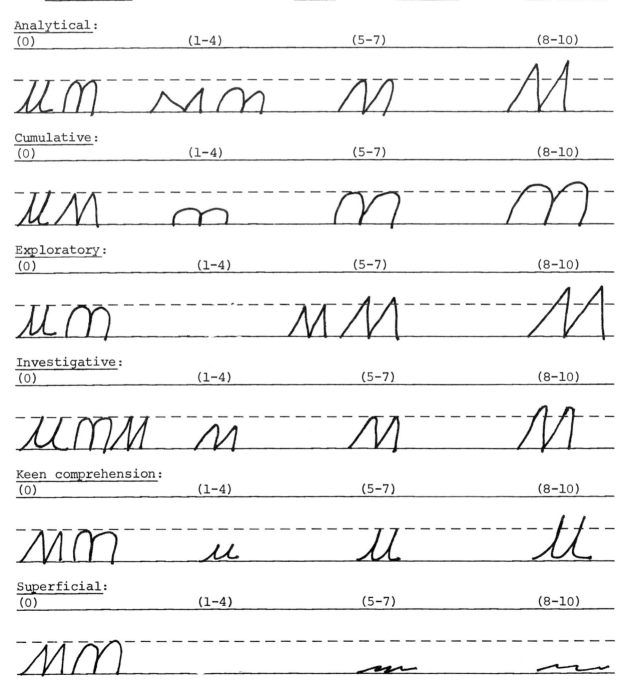

Analytical:
(0)   (1-4)   (5-7)   (8-10)

Cumulative:
(0)   (1-4)   (5-7)   (8-10)

Exploratory:
(0)   (1-4)   (5-7)   (8-10)

Investigative:
(0)   (1-4)   (5-7)   (8-10)

Keen comprehension:
(0)   (1-4)   (5-7)   (8-10)

Superficial:
(0)   (1-4)   (5-7)   (8-10)

<u>ANALYTICAL</u>:   (A primary trait)

<u>V-shaped</u> formation primarily seen in m's, n's, h's, and k's, but can be <u>found</u> <u>anywhere</u> in the <u>mundane</u> <u>area</u> of the writing. Major analytical = critical.

OPPOSITE: Gullible.

NO	(1-4)	(5-6)	(7-8)	(9-10)
mu	*mmm*	*M*	*M*	*M*

meyer   Commi   Main   team   mod

1-4   *time   the   and   mance*

5-6   *previous   am   longs*

7-8   *Tonight I'm taking my grand-*

9-10   *maybe   current.   money   Manager*
most

101

CUMULATIVE: (A primary trait)

Cumulative thinking is indicated by <u>rounded</u> or <u>flat-topped</u> m's, n's, and h's.

OPPOSITE: Keen comprehension.

NO	YES
mu	*m m h*

Thank-you
Hickman)   *might*   *my*

EXPLORATORY: (A primary trait)

Reversed or <u>inverted</u> "v" formation found primarily in m's, n's, and h's, but can be found anywhere in the mundane area. A stroke is a stroke.

<u>Must</u> be <u>as</u> <u>high</u> as the rest of the <u>mundane</u> <u>letters</u> to qualify. If lower, then it is investigative.

OPPOSITE: Superficial thinking.

NO	YES
mu	*M M h*

analysts   *want*   *Clui mbing*   *my*

required   *Brau*   *the*   *area*

INVESTIGATIVE THINKING: (A primary trait)

1. An exploratory stroke with a slightly rounded apex or top; can be higher, the same or lower than the rest of the mundane writing.

2. Or exploratory stroke which is not as high as the rest of the mundane writing.

It is the thinking process which lies between cumulative and exploratory; appears primarily in the m's, n's, and h's, but can be seen anywhere in the mundane area....a stroke is a stroke.

(0)	(1-4)	(5-7)	(8-10)

1-4

5-7

8-10

KEEN COMPREHENSION: (A primary trait)

A thinking process shown primarily in m's, n's, and h's that are made like
the small letter "i", or needle-point structures, but can be seen anywhere
in the mundane area.....a stroke is a stroke.

Intensity is determined by the amount of retracing and the height of the
stroke in relation to the rest of the mundane area height.

OPPOSITE: Cumulative thinking.

(0)	(1-4)	(5-7)	(8-10)

1-4   *is taken up and   we know.*

5-7   *I am   then find a time
        for retracing".*

8-10   *then come*

SUPERFICIAL THINKING: (A primary trait)

Shallow points on m's, n's and h's. Points are ill-formed and remain close
to the baseline. Could appear formless, spread out.

NO	SUPERFICIAL
Man	*man*

thinking: good

THINKING (MENTAL) PROCESSES, GOOD: (An evaluated trait)

The mental processes are as <u>high</u> or <u>higher</u> <u>than</u> the <u>rest</u> of the <u>mundane</u>
<u>letters</u> + <u>analytical</u> rating a <u>4</u> in intensity.

NO   THINKING GOOD

men.   *men*

firm beli
tests —

important

only accepts dr referrals - so am
calling Monday to see if I can
arrange that - receptionist said

thank Mrs Nancy
Hinton, on behalf of Julie's
grandmother + mother in par -

105

THINKING (MENTAL) PROCESSES, NOT GOOD :   (An evaluated trait)

Superficial thinking, or strokes that qualify for mental processes not rising as high as the rest of the mundane writing + lack of good analytical.

Check intensifiers and reductives to thinking before coming to conclusion of not good thinking.

Comment on thinking processes: Evaluating the thinking processes depends greatly on why the handwriting is being analyzed. For example, if you are working on an analysis for a person to be in a leadership position, then some exploratory and analytical is a must. So if the person does not have some exploratory/analytical thinking, then he or she will not be a good candidate for that job. Keen comprehension does not make a good teacher. So if this person is going to be in a position to teach or train others, then keen comprehension is not an asset. The cumulative thinker does not work well under pressure, or where problems need to be solved quickly on the spot.

GOOD	NOT GOOD THINKING
him	*him*

ensuing days
been bother
at Bethany
Ks

Besides doing ambula
was an orderly on
I placed people in

time at Dillion's Delicatessen

Kansas. My goals are to gain

I learning how to make my

as hard to do as it sounds.
enough. When I think of all the
known I was doing something

thrifty

<u>THRIFTY</u>:   (An evaluated trait)

<u>Conservative</u> + <u>no generosity</u>.

OPPOSITE: Extravagance.

NO	THRIFTY
given	*given*

...cause of the many organizations and individuals, leaders and elected officials who not only gave of..., but time and labor as well, keeping old landmarks in children and grandchildren to see, thereby pre-

...like a position in outside sales because of where I believe it lie. I feel lucky in having been hired by Thorpe the company is exactly what I was looking for, and the provided by Thorpe are important and very interesting to

with respect to Industrial Compressors. I also developed research skills and information retrieval systems in terms of the various OEM methods of cataloguing part numbers.

Carolina for 11 days. We're staying in tents at a campsite and driving down in a friends station wagon so our expenses are minimal. I know we'll have a great time. I've never been down that far south but a lot of my friends have and they say Myrtle Beach

107

TIMID: (An evaluated trait)

Clannish, conservative, self conscious, self underestimation, minor self confidence, selective, repression, reticence.

Intensifiers: Attention to details, caution, concentration, moderate to heavy depth, indecisive, jealousy, narrowminded, pessimism, precise, prejudice, procrastination, self deceit, sensitiveness, yielding, weak will power.

Reductives: Acquisitive, analytical, decisive, direct, dominating, enthusiasm, exploratory-investigative, high goals, initiative, organizational ability, persistence, tall philosophical loops, self confidence, showmanship, moderate to strong will power.

Concealers: Deceit, dignity, diplomacy, evasive, poise, vanity.

TOLERANT: (A primary trait)

Letter "e" made with a moderate loop. Intensified by moderately-sized philosophical loops.

NARROWMINDED	TOLERANT	BROADMINDED

ll   *l*   *l*

had her records and said she had no such check listed. She

clear across   splendid case
doesn't make

ULTRA CONSERVATIVE: (An evaluated trait)

Very narrow spacing between strokes (compressed, crowded, cramped strokes) +
writing has a tall look because of narrowness of letters and strokes.

Intensifiers: Attention to details, consistent slant, loyalty, organizational
ability, practical goals, pride, retracing (dignity, repression, very
restricted upper and lower loops), rhythm.

OPPOSITE: Generosity to self.

NO	ULTRA CONSERVATIVE
ultra	*ultra*

at Lackland Air
things of that self
bree from falling
lectures at the s
the service was

I want the job because
and Helsberg's growth rate
executives.

the opinions. The practice

products and services

UNREALISTIC DESIRE TO BE IMPORTANT: (A primary trait)

Misplaced capitals. <u>Words</u> <u>capitalized</u> that <u>need</u> <u>not</u> be <u>capitalized</u>.

NO	UNREALISTIC DESIRE TO BE IMPORTANT
letter that came	*letter That Came*

is achieved by those (W)ho (K)eep

My Favorite musicians are Earle

People Tend to Be Suspicious

We're still Remembering Our stay

Prejudice in South Africa. For his trouble arrested once again How many times has the been arrested While Speakin out for what nobody has been able to keep count Gregory always is in Jail Just as he always is a fast in order to make his point

<u>UNSTABLE</u>:   (An evaluated trait)

       <u>Baseline</u> <u>too</u> <u>uneven</u> + no determination + indecisive + <u>variable</u> <u>slant</u>.

VANITY: (A primary trait)

D- and t-stems at least 3 times the height of the mundane letters. The taller the stem, the more intensity rating of the trait. Stems can be looped or retraced.

Intensifiers: Deceit, domineering, ostentation, self confidence, self interest, self underestimation, sensitiveness, talkative, temper.

Reductives: Jealousy and L-structures taller than the vanity.

Evaluated vanity: Egotism + ostentation.

        (or)   vertical (AB) slant + jealousy + ostentation.

        (or)   Exaggerated philosophical imagination + pride.

<u>VARIABLE DEPTH</u>:   (A primary trait)

The smoothness or evenness of the depth of the writing is a plus in stability of the personality. Normally in writing, the downstrokes are slightly heavier than the upstrokes. If there is an obvious or strong difference in the depth of these strokes, then variable depth begins its count.

Usually variable depth is one that <u>varies</u> from <u>light</u> to <u>moderate</u> to <u>moderate</u> <u>heavy</u> <u>consistently</u> throughout the writing......or <u>upstrokes</u> heavier <u>than</u> the <u>downstrokes</u> in some letter formations.

VARIABLE SLANT: (An evaluated trait)

> Inconsistency in slant or several variations of slant (to the left, straight
> up, or to the right) and no one area predominates. When 100 measured
> consecutive upstrokes fall into 3 or more slant areas and no one area is
> predominant (at least 50 or more upstrokes falling into that area). For
> instance 20 FA, 20, AB, 20 BC, 20 CD, 20 E+. Or 10 FA, 30 AB, 30 CD, 30 DE.

*I attended Hutchinson High School. I gr
in 1964. I (Play all Varsity sports, I oo
Basketball, Baseball + track. I Went l n
to Hutchinson Jr College. after that I Sto*

*I would like to have   position of outside
mainly because of the opportunities to
meet different types of people. Having to deal
with customers & any problems they have,*

*a "readiness" stage has been reached wh
total background of experiences makes it p
him to quickly apply a new principle or
the solving of a problem - pg. 323*

VARIETY, DESIRE FOR: (A primary trait)

Active or exaggerated material imagination, as indicated in the lower loops.
The larger the loop, the more the desire for variety.

(0)	(1-4)	(5-7)	(8-10)
g	g	g	g

you improving has been salary

say good bye for Plumber, Yardman.

VERSATILE: (A primary trait)

Baseline varies, but smoothly.   Slightly bouncey or uneven baseline.

Straight baseline = rigid.

Baseline too bouncey or variable = unstable.

Intensifiers: Fluidity and keen comprehension.

*almost every Sunday. I told her
I was going to give you her
Name, if you would like t*

*Since could not find the stamina
to say goodbye to you each, I am
hoping this note will convey what*

*lead to a mature, experienced
a growth is the question for both
myself. I hope we can grow*

WILL POWER: (A primary trait)

    Indicated by the <u>weight</u> of the <u>t-bar</u> crossing in <u>relation</u> to the <u>lead-in</u> <u>stroke</u> of the <u>t-stem</u>. If t-stem is made with a direct stroke, check the t-bar with weight of the upstrokes in the writing.

    If t-bar crossing is lighter = weak will power.

    If t-bar crossing is the same weight = moderate will power.

    If t-bar crossing is heavier = strong will power.

LIGHT	MODERATE	STRONG
t	*t*	*t*
mast	*left –*	*started*

WIT: (An evaluated trait)

    Humor + sarcasm.

My paper is another Hard to

WITHDRAWAL: (A primary trait)

Left-slanted (FA) strokes in the slant + strokes in the writing made from right to left and that end or stay to the left.

Intensifiers: Clannish, deceit, no generosity, hesitation, broad or exaggerated philosophical imagination, indecisive, irritability, jealousy, repression, resentment, reticence, secrecy, selective, self conscious, self interest, selfish, sensitive, shallowness, stingy, stubborn, ultra conservative.

NO	WITHDRAWAL
yet if	*yet if*

WORRY: (A primary trait)

A reversed loop found in the m's, n's, h's, k's. An "upside-down" "e" formation.

NO	WORRY
m n h k	*m n h k*

YIELDINGNESS: (A primary trait)

    Found primarily in the <u>small</u> <u>letter</u> "<u>s</u>" when it is made with a <u>rounded</u>, soft stroke for a top instead of a usual, angular top. Secondary indication is in the letter "p" but can be seen in any letter formation.

(0)	(1-4)	(5-7)	(8-10)
◠	◠	◠	◠

1-4   *is so selected*

5-7   *list this is sufficient*

8-10   *references: was*

Part Two
Letters of the alphabet
and their traits

AREAS OF WRITING

PHILOSOPHICAL AREA: That portion of the writing that extends upward and higher than the mundane area, generally called the upper loops. The upper loop letters include the letters b, h, k, l, as well as the letters t and d and the upper portion of the letter f, traits of which letters fall into a philosophical or abstract/intangible area of personality.

MUNDANE AREA: The middle section of the writing that sits on the baseline of the writing. Normally the small letters a, c, e, i, m, n, o, r, s, u, v, w, and x are contained in this area. As are the first part of the letters d, g, j, p, q, y, and z; and as are the second part of the letters b, h, k, and p. Height of the mundane area letters = awareness, attention span.

MATERIAL AREA: That portion of the writing that extends below the baseline, consisting of a descending downstroke with or without a loop, generally called the lower loops. Normally the letters g, j, p, q, y, and z fall into this area, as does the lower portion of the letter f.

A. One of the circle letters.
    Falls into the mundane area.

_____ *a*   COMPULSIVE LIAR (double hook + loop)

_____ *a*   DECEIT (double loops)

_____ *a*   EVASIVE (hook within the circle)

_____ *a*   FRANK (clean, uncontaminated)

_____ *a*   SECRETIVE (loop on the right)

_____ *a*   SELF DECEIT (loop on the left)

_____ *a*   RETICENCE (closed at top)

_____ *a*   TALKATIVE (open at top)

B. Consists of an upper loop and a mundane area stroke. Falls into mundane and philosophical areas.

Loop width = amount of imagination

_____ LATENT (no loop, unfinished or unbased loop)

_____ RESTRICTED (slender, narrow loop)

_____ MODERATE (moderate loop)

_____ BROAD (larger loop)

_____ EXAGGERATED (very large loop)

Loop height = interest in things philosophical

_____ INTEREST IN THINGS PHILOSOPHICAL (tall loops, 2 1/2 times or taller than height of mundane area letters)

_____ PRACTICAL APPLICATION OR LACK OF INTEREST IN THINGS PHILOSOPHICAL (short loops, less than 2 times height of the mundane area letters)

_____ DIRECT (no lead-in stroke)

_____ RESENTMENT (straight lead-in stroke from baseline up)

_____ POSITIVE (straight stroke to baseline)

_____ TEMPER (tic at beginning of stroke)

_____ WARPED OR TWISTED PHILOSOPHY (waviness in loop)

_____ WITHDRAWAL (back-to-self ending stroke)

C

C. Falls into the mundane area.

_C_____ TEMPER (tic at beginning of stroke)

_C_____ COMPULSIVE LIAR (double hook + loop); intensifies trait when found in this letter in addition to in circle letters.

D. Consists of a circle formation connected to an upper extender. Falls into the mundane and philosophical areas.

_d_____ COMPULSIVE LIAR (double hook + loop)

_d_____ EVASIVE (hook within the circle)

_d_____ FRANK (clean, uncontaminated)

_d_____ SELF DECEIT (loop on left of circle)

_d_____ TALKS ABOUT SELF (open circle)

_d_____ DIGNITY (retraced stem)

_d_____ EMPATHY (slender, narrow looped stem)

_d_____ MODERATE SENSITIVENESS (moderately looped stem)

_d_____ STRONG SENSITIVENESS (large looped stem)

_d_____ STUBBORN (wedged stem)

_d_____ DELIBERATE (separated stem)

_d_____ DIRECT (no lead-in stroke)

_d_____ CULTURE (Delta D)

_d d_____ INDEPENDENT (height less than 2 times mundane)

_d d_____ PRIDE (height 2 to 2 3/4 times mundane)

_d d_____ VANITY (height 3 times or taller than mundane)

E. A small loop. Falls into the
mundane area.

BROADMINDED (well rounded loop)

TOLERANT (moderate loop)

NARROWMINDED (narrow or closed loop)

CULTURE (Greek E)

GENEROSITY (long final)

GENEROSITY, EXTREME (very long final)

RESENTMENT (straight lead-in stroke from baseline)

F. Consists of an upper loop and
a lower loop. Falls into the
mundane, philosophical and the
material areas.

ORGANIZATIONAL ABILITY
(balanced stem above
and below baseline)

NOT ORGANIZED (not
balanced above and
below baseline)

PHILOSOPHICAL INTEREST
(tall upper loop)

DETERMINATION
(straight downstroke
below baseline)

DIRECT (no lead-in
stroke)

FLUIDITY (figure 8)

PERSISTENCE (tie
formation)

POSITIVE (straight
downstroke above
baseline)

WITHDRAWAL (back-
to-self ending
stroke)

<u>G</u>. Consists of a circle formation, a downstroke below the baseline
and a lower loop. Falls into the mundane and material areas.

<u>Circle formations</u>:

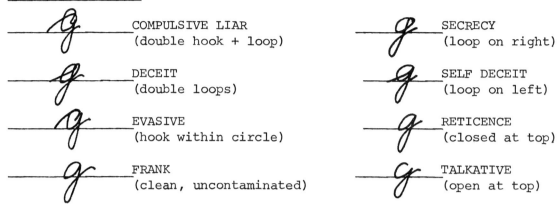

COMPULSIVE LIAR
(double hook + loop)

SECRECY
(loop on right)

DECEIT
(double loops)

SELF DECEIT
(loop on left)

EVASIVE
(hook within circle)

RETICENCE
(closed at top)

FRANK
(clean, uncontaminated)

TALKATIVE
(open at top)

<u>DETERMINATION</u> = straight downstroke below baseline:

Weight = strength

Length = endurance

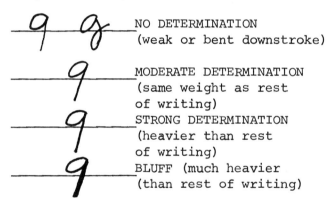

NO DETERMINATION
(weak or bent downstroke)

MODERATE DETERMINATION
(same weight as rest
of writing)

STRONG DETERMINATION
(heavier than rest
of writing)

BLUFF (much heavier
(than rest of writing)

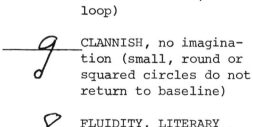

ROUTINE (short, less
than 2 times mundane
height)

MODERATE (2 to 3 times
mundane height)

DESIRE FOR CHANGE
(long, more than 3
times height of the
mundane)

<u>IMAGINATION MATERIAL</u> = Completed loops:

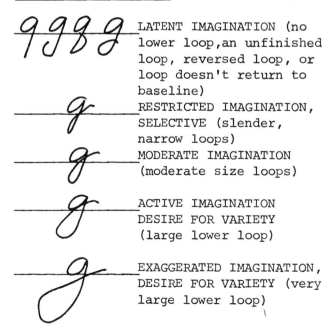

LATENT IMAGINATION (no
lower loop, an unfinished
loop, reversed loop, or
loop doesn't return to
baseline)

RESTRICTED IMAGINATION,
SELECTIVE (slender,
narrow loops)

MODERATE IMAGINATION
(moderate size loops)

ACTIVE IMAGINATION
DESIRE FOR VARIETY
(large lower loop)

EXAGGERATED IMAGINATION,
DESIRE FOR VARIETY (very
large lower loop)

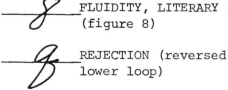

AGGRESSIVE, no imag-
ination (break-away
from downstroke, no
loop)

CLANNISH, no imagina-
tion (small, round or
squared circles do not
return to baseline)

FLUIDITY, LITERARY
(figure 8)

REJECTION (reversed
lower loop)

WITHDRAWAL (back-to-
self ending stroke)

H. Consists of an upper loop and a thinking process formation. Falls into the mundane and philosophical areas.

Loop width = amount of philosophical interest

LATENT (no loop, unfinished or unbased loop)

RESTRICTED (slender, narrow loop)

MODERATE (moderate loop)

BROAD (larger loop)

EXAGGERATED (very large loop)

DIRECT (no lead-in stroke)

INITIATIVE (break-away stroke)

LEARNING DISABILITY (3 points of letter not all returning or touching baseline)

POSITIVE (straight stroke to baseline)

REPRESSION (retraced upstroke)

WARPED OR TWISTED PHILOSOPHY (waviness in loop)

WORRY (upside-down e-loop)

Loop height = interest in things philosophical

INTEREST IN THINGS PHILOSOPHICAL (tall loop, 2 1/2 times or taller than height of mundane)

PRACTICAL APPLICATION OR LACK OF INTEREST IN THINGS PHILOSOPHICAL (short loop, less than 2 times height of the mundane)

ANALYTICAL (v-formation at baseline)

CUMULATIVE (rounded top)

EXPLORATORY (inverted V, sharp point at top)

INVESTIGATIVE (slightly rounded apex)

KEEN (retraced upstroke)

SUPERFICIAL (close to baseline)

I. Consists of a stem and a dot. Stem falls
into mundane area, dots fall into philosophical area.

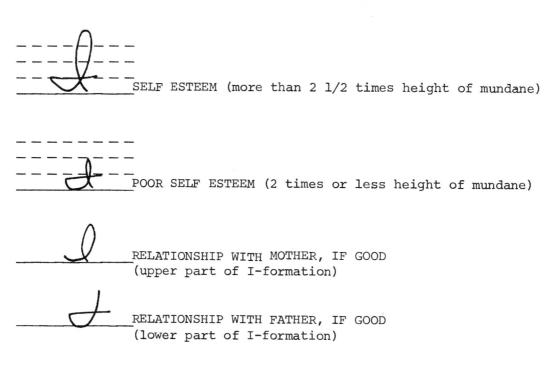

i ATTENTION TO DETAILS
(dot close to stem)

i MODERATE ATTENTION
TO DETAILS (dot slightly
away from stem)

i INATTENTION TO DETAILS
(dot far away from stem
or missing altogether)

i IDIOSYNCRACY
(circle i-dot)

i IRRITABILITY
(jabbed/slashed dot)

i PROCRASTINATION IN
LITTLE THINGS (dot
to left of stem)

i LOYALTY
(round dot)

CAPITAL I.

SELF ESTEEM (more than 2 1/2 times height of mundane)

POOR SELF ESTEEM (2 times or less height of mundane)

RELATIONSHIP WITH MOTHER, IF GOOD
(upper part of I-formation)

RELATIONSHIP WITH FATHER, IF GOOD
(lower part of I-formation)

ℐ -insecure

*ℐ - interruption in relationship w/ male parent.
Physical or emotional separation between mother & father.*

J. Consists of a stem in the mundane area, a downstroke and lower loop in the material area and a dot in the philosophical area.

j ATTENTION TO DETAILS (dot close to stem

j MODERATE ATTENTION TO DETAILS (dot slightly away from stem)

j INATTENTION TO DETAILS (dot far away or missing from stem)

j IDIOSYNCRACY (circle i-dot)

j IRRITABILITY (jabbed/slashed dot)

j PROCRASTINATION IN LITTLE THINGS (dot to left of stem)

j LOYALTY (round dot)

DETERMINATION = straight downstroke below baseline:

Weight = strength

j NO DETERMINATION (weak or bent downstroke)

j MODERATE DETERMINATION (same weight as rest of writing)

j STRONG DETERMINATION (heavier than rest of writing)

j BLUFF (much heavier than rest of writing)

Length = endurance

j ROUTINE (short, less than 2 times mundane height)

j MODERATE (2 to 3 times mundane height)

j DESIRE FOR CHANGE (long, more than 3 times height of the mundane)

j AGGRESSIVE, no imagination (break-away from downstroke, no loop)

j CLANNISH, no imagination (small, round or squared circles do not return to baseline)

j FLUIDITY, LITERARY (figure 8)

j REJECTION (reversed lower loop)

j WITHDRAWAL (back-to-self ending stroke) **128**

IMAGINATION MATERIAL = Completed loops:

jjjj LATENT IMAGINATION (no lower loop, an unfinished loop, reversed loop, or loop doesn't return to baseline)

j RESTRICTED IMAGINATION, SELECTIVE (slender, narrow loop)

j MODERATE IMAGINATION (moderate size loops)

j ACTIVE IMAGINATION, DESIRE FOR VARIETY (large lower loop)

j EXAGGERATED IMAGINATION, DESIRE FOR VARIETY (very large lower loop)

K. Consists of an upper loop and a buckle in the
mundane area. Falls into the philosophical and
mundane areas.

Loop width = amount of imagination

LATENT (no loop,
unfinished or
unbased loop)

RESTRICTED
(slender, narrow
loop)

MODERATE
(moderate loop)

BROAD (larger
loop)

EXAGGERATED
(very large loop)

DIRECT
(no lead-in stroke)

INITIATIVE
(break-away stroke)

POSITIVE (stroke
straight to baseline)

REPRESSION
(retraced upstroke)

RESENTMENT (straight
lead-in from baseline)

TEMPER (tic at beginning
of stroke)

WARPED OR TWISTED
PHILOSOPHY (waviness in
loop)

WORRY
(upside-down e-loop)

Loop height = interest in things
philosophical

INTEREST IN THINGS
PHILOSOPHICAL (tall
loop, 2 1/2 times or
taller than height of
mundane)

PRACTICAL APPLICATION
OR LACK OF INTEREST
IN THINGS PHILOSOPHI-
CAL (short loop, less
than 2 times height
of mundane)

ANALYTICAL
(v-formation)

DEFIANCE (buckle or
s-structure rises
above mundane
letters)

L. An upper loop. Falls into
the philosophical area.

Loop width = amount of imagination

LATENT (no loop, unfinished loop, or unbased loop)

RESTRICTED (slender, narrow loop)

MODERATE (moderate loop)

BROAD (larger loop)

EXAGGERATED (very large loop)

Loop height = interest in things philosophical

INTEREST IN THINGS PHILOSOPHICAL (tall loops, 2 1/2 times or
taller than height of mundane area)

PRACTICAL APPLICATION OR LACK OF INTEREST IN THINGS PHILOSOPHICAL
(short loops, less than 2 times height of mundane area)

DIRECT (no lead-in stroke)

POSITIVE (stroke straight to baseline)

TEMPER (tic at beginning of stroke)

WARPED OR TWISTED PHILOSOPHY (waviness in loop)

M and N.   Contain mental or thinking processes.
Fall into the mundane area.

_____ANALYTICAL (v-formation)

_____CUMULATIVE (rounded top)

_____EXPLORATORY (inverted v-formation, sharp pointed top)

_____INVESTIGATIVE (slightly rounded apex)

_____KEEN (retraced points)

_____SUPERFICIAL (stays close to baseline)

_____SELF CONSCIOUS (last hump taller than rest)

_____DIPLOMACY (letter tapers 3 times)

_____LEARNING DISABILITY (3 points not returning evenly or all not touching baseline)

_____REPRESSION (retracing of downstroke)

_____WORRY (reversed loop, upside-down e-formation)

_____HUMOR (initial flourish)

_____DRY HUMOR (lead-in at angle and attached to downstroke)

_____TEMPER (tic at beginning of stroke)

_____NEED FOR LOVE & AFFECTION (final portion of M or N contains hook)

O

O. One of the circle letters; falls in the mundane area.

_____ COMPULSIVE LIAR (double hook + loop)

_____ DECEIT (double loops)

_____ EVASIVE (initial hook within circle)

_____ FRANK (clean, uncontaminated)

_____ SECRECY (loop on the right)

_____ SELF DECEIT (loop on the left)

_____ RETICENCE (closed at top)

_____ TALKATIVE (open at top)

_____ RESENTMENT (inflexible lead-in stroke)

132

P

P. Falls into the mundane and material areas;
may extend into philosophical area.

Downstroke = determination (if straight)

WEAK DETERMINATION (lighter than rest of writing)

MODERATE DETERMINATION (same weight as rest of writing)

STRONG DETERMINATION (heavier than rest of writing)

Loop size = mental desire for physical activity

PRECISE (loop retraced)

RESTRICTED DESIRE FOR PHYSICAL ACTIVITY
(slender, narrow loop)

MODERATE DESIRE FOR PHYSICAL ACTIVITY
(moderate size loop)

STRONG DESIRE FOR PHYSICAL ACTIVITY
(large size loop)

Upper part of "P":

YIELDING (soft or rounded top structure)

SLIGHTLY ARGUMENTATIVE (lead-in slightly higher than mundane)

ARGUMENTATIVE (lead-in twice as high as mundane)

VERY ARGUMENTATIVE (lead-in more than 2 times height of
mundane)

DIRECT (no lead-in stroke)

EXPLORES IDEAS TO ARGUE ABOUT (exploratory top)

IMAGINES THINGS TO ARGUE ABOUT (moderate or large loop at top)

Q. Consists of a circle formation and
a descending downstroke with a lower
loop. Falls into mundane and the
material areas.

Circle portion:

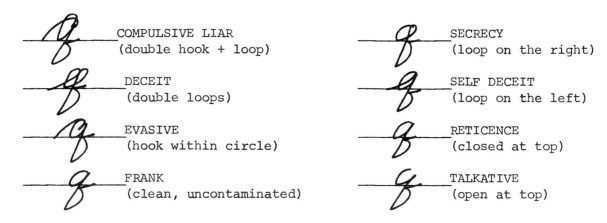

COMPULSIVE LIAR
(double hook + loop)

DECEIT
(double loops)

EVASIVE
(hook within circle)

FRANK
(clean, uncontaminated)

SECRECY
(loop on the right)

SELF DECEIT
(loop on the left)

RETICENCE
(closed at top)

TALKATIVE
(open at top)

NO EVALUATION OF IMAGINATION is made of the letter Q, since the loop is made
backward from an imagination loop and is its normal formation.

<u>Determination</u> = straight downstroke descending from baseline

Weight = strength

Length = endurance

NO DETERMINATION
(weak or bent downstroke)

MODERATE DETERMINATION
(same weight as rest
of writing)

STRONG DETERMINATION
(heavier than rest
of writing)

BLUFF (much heavier
than rest of writing

ROUTINE (short, less
than twice height of
mundane letters)

MODERATE (2 to 3 times
height of mundane)

DESIRE FOR CHANGE
(long, more than 3
times height of the
mundane)

PERSISTENCE (tie
formation)

R. Falls into the mundane area.

_____ ANALYTICAL
        (v-formation)

_____ CUMULATIVE
        (rounded top)

_____ EXPLORATORY
        (inverted v-formation)

_____ INVESTIGATIVE
        (slightly rounded apex)

_____ KEEN (needle pointed)

_____ CULTURE
        (made like Greek E)

_____ MANUAL DEXTERITY
        (flat-topped)

_____ REPRESSION
        (retraced downstroke)

_____ TENACITY
        (final hook)

_____ NEED TO BE CREATIVE WITH
        HANDS ("R" rises above
        the rest of the letters)
        *Writer is not using
         hands enough to satisfy
         his creative urges.

S. Falls into mundane area.

_____ NO YIELDING
        (pointed at top)

_____ YIELDING
        (soft, rounded top)

_____ FLUIDITY
        (figure 8 structure)

_____ PERSISTENCE
        (tie formation)

T. Falls into the mundane and/or philosophical areas.

STEM HEIGHT:

INDEPENDENT
(short, less than 2 times mundane height)

BARE PRIDE
(2 times height of mundane)

PRIDE
(2 1/2 times mundae height)

VANITY
(3 or more times height of mundane)

STEM LOOP:

DIGNITY
(retraced stem)

EMPATHY
(slightly looped stem)

SENSITIVE
(moderate to large loop)

DELIBERATE
(stem separated)

DIRECT
(no lead-in stroke)

POSITIVE
(straight to baseline)

STUBBORN
(wedge-shaped stem)

T-CROSSINGS or T-BARS:

Will Power:

WEAK WILL POWER
(bar lighter than lead-in stroke)
MODERATE WILL POWER
(bar same weight as lead-in stroke)
STRONG WILL POWER
(bar heavier than lead-in stroke)

Goals: (stem must be minimum of 2 times height of mundane area)

VISIONARY
(above stem)

DISTANT
(at top of stem)

HIGH PRACTICAL
(3/4 way up stem)

PRACTICAL
(midway up stem)

LIMITED
(same height as mundane)

LOW
(below top of mundane)

SELF UNDERESTIMATION
(limited or low goals)

T (continued)

T. <u>T-Crossings</u> or <u>T-Bars</u> (continued)

t   DOMINATING
(heavier as it goes downward)

t   DOMINEERING
(downward with feathered ending)

t   ENTHUSIASM
(long or longer than stem is tall)

th   FLUIDITY
(t-bar flows/connects with next letter)

t   IMPATIRNCE
(t-bar to right of stem and touching)

t   OPTIMISM
(t-bar slants upward)

t   PERSISTENCE
(t-bat tie formation)

t   PRECISE
(t-bar short, carefully balanced)

t t   PROCRASTINATION
(t-bar to left of stem)

t   SELF CASTIGATION
(t-bar crosses from right to left)

t   SELF CONTROL
(t-bar bent)

t   SHALLOW
(t-bar dish-shaped)

t   TEMPER
(t-bar to right of stem, not touching)

U, V, W, X. Fall into the mundane area.

Mental or thinking processes:

_____ANALYTICAL (v-formation)

_____CUMULATIVE (rounded top)

_____EXPLORATORY (inverted V, sharp pointed top)

_____INVESTIGATIVE (slightly rounded apex)

_____KEEN (retraced point)

_____SUPERFICIAL (stays close to baseline)

W. (only)

_____DIPLOMACY (strokes taper 3 times)

_____SELF CONSCIOUS (last stroke higher than rest)

_____HUMOR (initial flourish)

_____DRY HUMOR (lead-in at angle and attached to downstroke)

Y. Falls into the mundane and material areas. Consists of a portion that may indicate thinking processes and a descending downstroke with or without a lower loop.

Mundane portion:

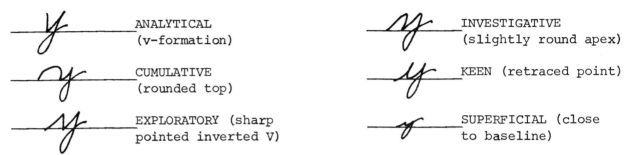

ANALYTICAL (v-formation)

INVESTIGATIVE (slightly round apex)

CUMULATIVE (rounded top)

KEEN (retraced point)

EXPLORATORY (sharp pointed inverted V)

SUPERFICIAL (close to baseline)

DETERMINATION = straight downstroke below baseline:

Weight = strength

Length = endurance

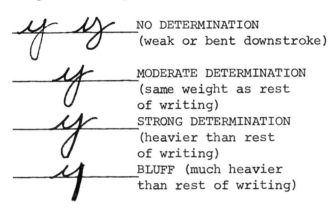

NO DETERMINATION (weak or bent downstroke)

ROUTINE (short, less than 2 times height of mundane)

MODERATE DETERMINATION (same weight as rest of writing)

MODERATE (2 to 3 times height of mundane)

STRONG DETERMINATION (heavier than rest of writing)

BLUFF (much heavier than rest of writing)

DESIRE FOR CHANGE (long, more than 3 times height of mundane)

IMAGINATION MATERIAL = completed loops:

LATENT IMAGINATION (no lower loop, an unfinished loop, reversed loop, or loop doesn't return to baseline)

AGGRESSIVE, no imagination (break-away from downstroke, no loop)

RESTRICTED IMAGINATION, SELECTIVE (slender, narrow loops)

CLANNISH, no imagination (small, round or squared circles do not return to baseline)

MODERATE IMAGINATION (moderate size loops)

FLUIDITY, LITERARY (figure 8)

ACTIVE IMAGINATION, DESIRE FOR VARIETY, (large lower loops)

REJECTION (reversed lower loop)

EXAGGERATED IMAGINATION, DESIRE FOR VARIETY (very large lower loops)

WITHDRAWAL (back-to-self ending stroke)

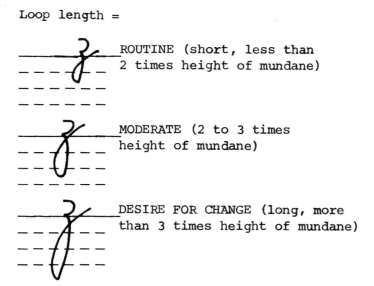

Z. Falls into mundane and material areas.

Loop length =

_____ ROUTINE (short, less than 2 times height of mundane)

_____ MODERATE (2 to 3 times height of mundane)

_____ DESIRE FOR CHANGE (long, more than 3 times height of mundane)

IMAGINATION MATERIAL = Completed loops:

NO IMAGINATION (no lower loop, an unfinished loop, reversed loop, or loop that doesn't return to baseline)

RESTRICTED IMAGINATION, SELECTIVE (slender, narrow loops)

MODERATE IMAGINATION (moderate size loops)

ACTIVE IMAGINATION, DESIRE FOR VARIETY (large lower loop)

EXAGGERATED IMAGINATION, DESIRE FOR VARIETY (very large lower loop)

AGGRESSIVE, no imagination (break-away from downstroke, no loop)

CLANNISH, no imagination (small, round or squared circles do not return to baseline)

FLUIDITY, LITERARY (figure 8)

REJECTION (reversed lower loop)

WITHDRAWAL (back-to-self ending stroke)

Beginning Strokes

BEGINNING STROKES: Can be seen on any letter.

t — ACQUISITIVE (initial hook)

to — DIRECT (no lead-in stroke)

h — HESITATION (long lead-in stroke)

m — HUMOR (lead-in flourish)

m — DRY HUMOR (stroke at angle and attached to downstroke)

m — JEALOUSY (small inverted circle)

m — RESPONSIBILITY, DESIRE FOR (large inverted circle)

a — RESENTMENT (inflexible lead-in from baseline)

t — TEMPER (tic at beginning of stroke)

m ← fear of being hurt by o

ENDING STROKES: Can be seen on any letter.

end — CAUTION (line used to fill out a line of writing)

t — DECISIVE (firm, blunt ending)

e — DESIRE FOR ATTENTION (last stroke raises higher than mundane)

y — FATALISM (drooping final stroke at end of word)

e — GENEROSITY (long final)

e — GENEROSITY, EXTREME (very long final)

a — INDECISIVE (ending feathers out)

& — MATTER OF FACT (downslant on final)

e — OPTIMISM (upward slanted ending stroke)

t — SARCASM (t-bar ending feathers out)

ty — TENACITY (final hook)

d — WALK OVER OTHERS (strong downward slanted final)

Part Three
Trait Intensity Chart

TRAIT INTENSITY CHART

Trait	Description	0	1-2	3-4	5-6	7-8	9-10	Count Determines Intensity
ACQUISITIVE	initial hook							
AGGRESSIVE	breakaway below the baseline							
ANALYTICAL	v-formations							
ARGUMENTATIVE	high lead-in stroke in p's							
ATTENTION, DESIRE FOR	high ending strokes							
ATTENTION TO DETAILS	closely dotted i's							
BROADMINDED	open e's							
CHANGE, DESIRE FOR	long downstroke 3 times mundane height							
CLANNISHNESS	small loop at bottom of down-stroke							
COMPULSIVE LIAR	figure 8 on top of circle letter							

Trait	Description	0	1-2	3-4	5-6	7-8	9-10	Count Determines Intensity
CONCENTRATION	small writing	*large*				*small*		✓
CONSERVATIVE	close spacing of letters	*con*			*conser*	*conden*	*conden*	
CUMULATIVE	rounded m's, n's, h's	*m m*			*m*	*m*	*m*	
DAY DREAMING	t-bars above stem	*t t to to*			*t to*			✓
DECEIT	double loop in a's, o's, g's	*o*	*o*	*o*	*o*	*o*	*o*	
DECISIVE	blunt endings	*t*			*t*		*t*	
DEFIANCE	buckle of "k" rises high	*k k*	*k k*	*k k*	*k k*	*k k*	*k k*	
DELIBERATE	separated stems	*t d*			*d t*			✓
DETERMINATION	downstrokes below baseline	*g y*			*g y*	*g y*	*g y*	
DIGNITY	retraced t- and d- stems	*t d*			*t d to d*	*t d to d*		✓

144

TRAIT INTENSITY CHART

Trait	Description	0	1-2	3-4	5-6	7-8	9-10	Count Determines Intensity
DIPLOMACY	letter tapers downward	*m m*			*m*		*m*	
DIRECTNESS	no approach stroke	*t k*			*to be h*			✓
DOMINATING	t-bar slants forward & down	*t*			*t*			✓
DOMINEERING	downward t-bar & feathered end	*t*			*t*			✓
ENTHUSIASM	t-bar longer than stem high	*t*			*t*	*t t*		
EVASIVE	initial hook within circle	*a*			*a*		*a*	
EXPLORATORY	inverted "v" in m's, n's, h's	*mu*			*m*	*m m*	*m*	
FATALISM	drooping end on final stroke	*gf*			*g*	*g*		✓
FLUIDITY	figure-8 g's, fluid f's, t-bars connect	*th f g*			*th f 8*			✓
FRANK	clean circle letters	*a a a*			*a*			✓

145

Trait	Description	0	1-2	3-4	5-6	7-8	9-10	Count Determines Intensity
GENEROSITY	long finals	*(handwriting)*			*(handwriting)*	*(handwriting)*	*(handwriting)*	
GENEROSITY, EXTREME	very long finals				*(handwriting)*	*(handwriting)*	*(handwriting)*	
GOALS, VISIONARY	t-bars above stem				*(handwriting)*			✓
GOALS, DISTANT	t-bar at top of stem				*(handwriting)*			✓
GOALS, HIGH PRACTICAL	t-bar 2/3 way up stem				*(handwriting)*			✓
GOALS, PRACTICAL	t-bar 1/2 way up stem				*(handwriting)*			✓
GOALS, LIMITED	t-bar at top of mundane				*(handwriting)*			✓
GOALS, LOW	t-bar lower than mundane				*(handwriting)*			✓
HUMOR	lead-in flourish	*(handwriting)*			*(handwriting)*			✓
IDIOSYNCRACY	circle i-dots	*(handwriting)*			*(handwriting)*			✓

TRAIT INTENSITY CHART

Trait	Description	0	1-2	3-4	5-6	7-8	9-10	Count Determines Intensity
IMAGINATION, MATERIAL	loops below baseline							
IMAGINATION, PHILOSOPHICAL	loops above baseline							
IMPATIENCE	t-bar touching & right of stem							✓
IMPRACTICAL	t-bars all low OR ALL HIGH							✓
INDECISIVE	t-bar feathers out at end							✓
INDEPENDENT	short t- and d- stems							✓
INITIATIVE	breakaway from baseline							
INTUITION	breaks between letters of word							✓
INVESTIGATIVE	short or rounded apex, inverted v							
IRRITABILITY	jabs or dashes for i-dots							

Trait	Description	0	1-2	3-4	5-6	7-8	9-10	Count Determines Intensity
JEALOUSY	small initial loop	*I m*			*I m*			✓
KEEN	needle-pointed m's, n's, h's	*m*	*m*	*m*	*m*	*m*	*m*	
LARGE WRITING	mundane 3/16" or larger	*small*			*large*			
LITERARY	Greek E, figure 8's, delta D				$\varepsilon, 8, \mathcal{g}, \partial$			✓
LOYALTY	round i-dots	*i i*			*i*			✓
MANUAL DEXTERITY	flat-topped "r" structures	*r*			*π*			✓
NARROWMINDED	narrow or closed e's	*e e*			*e e*			✓
ORGANIZATION ABILITY	balanced f's	*f f*			*f f*		*f*	✓
PERSISTENCE	tie formation	*f t*			*f t*			✓

TRAIT INTENSITY CHART

Trait	Description	0	1-2	3-4	5-6	7-8	9-10	Count Determines Intensity
PESSIMISM	downslanted lines	*(optimism)*				*(pessimism)*		
PHILOSOPHY, INTEREST IN	tall upper loops							
PHYSICAL-MINDEDNESS	loop size in letter "p"							
POSITIVE	straight line to baseline							✓
PRACTICAL	t-bars midway on stem							✓
PRECISE	retraced p-stem, close i-dots, short t-bars							✓
PRIDE	t-stems 2 1/2 times tall							✓
PROCRAST-INATION	t-bar on left of stem							✓
REPRESSION	retracing of a downstroke							
RESENTMENT	inflexible lead-in stroke							

149

Trait	Description	0	1-2	3-4	5-6	7-8	9-10	Count Determines Intensity
RESPONSIBILITY, DESIRE FOR	large initial loop	*m*			*m*			✓
RETICENCE	closed circles	*a o a*			*a o*	*a*		✓
SARCASM	pointed t-bar	*t*			*t*	*d*		✓
SECRETIVE	loop on right of circle	*o a*	*o*	*o*	*a*	*a*	*a*	
SELECTIVE	slender lower loop	*y g*			*y g*			✓
SELF CASTIGATION	t-bar made right to left	*t*			*d*			✓
SELF CONSCIOUS	final hump on "m" rises high	*m*	*m*	*m*	*m*	*m*	*m*	
SELF CONTROL	bowed t-bar	*t t*	*t*	*t*	*t*	*t*	*t*	
SELF DECEIT	loop on left of circle	*a d*	*a*	*a*	*a*	*a*	*a*	
SELF ESTEEM	capital 2 1/2 times mundane.	*Di*			*Di*	*Di*	*Di Di Di*	

150

TRAIT INTENSITY CHART

Trait	Description	0	1-2	3-4	5-6	7-8	9-10	Count Determines Intensity
SELF RELIANT	underscore	*Mary*			*Mary*			
SELF UNDER-ESTIMATION	low t-bars	*t, t, to, to*				*t*		
SENSITIVENESS	looped t- and d- stems	*t d*	*t d*	*t d*	*t d*	*t d*	*t d*	
SHALLOW	basin-shaped t-bars	*t*			*t*	*t*	*t*	
STUBBORN	wedged t- and d- stems	*d t*			*t d*	*t d*	*t d*	∨
SUPERFICIAL	m's, n's, close to baseline	*m n*			*m*			∨
TALKATIVE	open circle	*a o*	*a*	*a*	*a*	*a*	*a*	
TEMPER	t-bar on right or initial tic	*t*			*t b*			
TENACITY	final hook	*t*			*t, g*	*g*		∨
THINKING, ANALYTICAL	v-formations	*m n*			*m n m*	*m m*	*m*	
THINKING, CUMULATIVE	rounded tops	*m m*			*m m*	*m m*	*m*	
THINKING, EXPLORATORY	inverted "v"	*m m*			*m*	*m m*	*m*	

151

Trait	Description	0	1-2	3-4	5-6	7-8	9-10	Count Determines Intensity
THINKING, INVESTIGATIVE	low exploratory or rounded apex	*MM*		*M*	*M*	*M*	*M*	
THINKING, KEEN	needle-points	*MM*		*u*	*M*	*M*	*M*	
THINKING, SUPERFICIAL	stays close to baseline	*MM*			*~*			
TOLERANT	"e" made with moderate loop	*e e*			*e*			✓
ULTRA CONSERVATIVE	very close spacing	*met*			*ultraconservator*			
VANITY	t- and d-stems over 2 1/2 times mundane height	*t d d*	*t*	*t*	*t d t d d*	*t f l t d d d*	*t*	✓
VARIETY, DESIRE FOR	large lower loops	*g g y g*			*y g y g*	*y g g g*	*y*	
WILL POWER	weight of t-bar		*t*	*t*	*t*	*t*	*t*	
WORRY	upside-down "e" in m's, n's, h's	*MM*			*ee*			✓
YIELDING	soft s's, p's	*p*		*p*	*p*	*p*	*p*	

152

Notes:

Notes:

Notes: